D A

Spokane

Arctic

W9-BVN-139

Brooks Range

• Ft. Yukon

Bering

Sea

YUKON R.

A L A S K A

• Fairbanks

Wallowas

Middle Fork
of the Salmon

SALMON R.

MT. McGUIRE

Salmon
City

EAGLE CAP

MIDDLE FORK

• Stanley

TAHOE L.

The High Sierra

RITTER
PEAK →

MONO L.

DEVIL POSTPILE

GREAT

OWENS VALLEY

Boise

CENTRAL
• Fresno

MT. WHITNEY →

I D A H O

VALLEY

• Lone Pine

OWENS L.

SNAKE R.

C A L I F O R N I A

map by palacios

MY WILDERNESS
THE PACIFIC WEST

BY WILLIAM O. DOUGLAS

My Wilderness: The Pacific West
America Challenged
West of the Indus
The Right of the People
Russian Journey
We the Judges
An Almanac of Liberty
North From Malaya
Beyond the High Himalayas
Strange Lands and Friendly People
Of Men and Mountains

MY WILDERNESS

THE PACIFIC WEST

William O. Douglas

ILLUSTRATIONS BY FRANCIS LEE JAQUES

1960
DOUBLEDAY & COMPANY, INC.
GARDEN CITY, NEW YORK

Library of Congress Catalog Card Number 60–13519
Copyright © 1960 by William O. Douglas
All Rights Reserved
Printed in the United States of America
First Edition

"In God's wildness lies the hope of the world—
the great fresh unblighted, unredeemed wilderness.
The galling harness of civilization drops off, and the
wounds heal ere we are aware."

JOHN MUIR, *Alaska Fragment* 1890.

"* * * if I should be fated to walk no more with
Nature, be compelled to leave all I most devoutly
love in the wilderness, return to civilization and be
twisted into the characterless cable of society, then
these sweet, free, cumberless rovings will be as
chinks and slits on life's horizon, through which I
may obtain glimpses of the treasures that lie in God's
wilds beyond my reach."

JOHN MUIR, *Notes* (1873)

"We must be refreshed by the sight of inexhaustible vigor . . .
the wilderness with its living and its decaying trees
the thunder cloud and the rain . . .
some life pasturing freely where we never wander."

Thoreau, *Walden* (1854)

CONTENTS

CHAPTER I

BROOKS RANGE

THE Arctic has strange stillness that no other wilderness knows. It has loneliness too—a feeling of isolation and remoteness born of vast spaces, the rolling tundra, and the barren domes of limestone mountains. This is a loneliness that is joyous and exhilarating. All the noises of civilization have been left behind; now the music of the wilderness can be heard. The Arctic shows beauty in this bareness and in the shadows cast by clouds over empty land. The beauty is in part the glory of seeing moose,

9

caribou, and wolves living in a natural habitat, untouched by civilization. It is the thrill of seeing birds come thousands of miles to nest and raise their young. The beauty is also in slopes painted cerise by a low-bush rhododendron, in strange mosses and lichens that grow everywhere, and (to one who gets on his hands and knees) in the glories of delicate saxifrage, arctic poppies, and fairy forget-me-nots. The Arctic has a call that is compelling. The distant mountains make one want to go on and on over the next ridge and over the one beyond. The call is that of a wilderness known only to a few. It is a call to adventure. This is not a place to possess like the plateaus of Wyoming or the valleys of Arizona; it is one to behold with wonderment. It is a domain for any restless soul who yearns to discover the startling beauties of creation in a place of quiet and solitude where life exists without molestation by man.

I was sitting under a white spruce on the upper reaches of the Sheenjek River in the Brooks Range of Alaska. Our camp was at 68° 36′ N., 143° 45′ W. Glaciers estimated to be 1400 feet thick once moved over this country. Only a few remnants of them are left and they are at the very head of the Sheenjek. But their work is evident on every hand. The mountain ridges are rounded and polished; the valley is U-shaped; morainal deposits cover the valley floor; potholes dot the area.

We were camped on one pothole filled with dark blue water and over 200 acres in size. It lies at an elevation of about 2000 feet. It is the last one up the Sheenjek Valley large enough for a seaplane to negotiate. And therefore Olaus J. Murie, biologist and conservationist, and his wife Mardy, who were heading a scientific expedition into these mountains, appropriately called it Last Lake.

I sat for an hour or more under my spruce tree. The first friend to approach was an arctic ground squirrel. He was a quiet body, not chattering or scolding like our western species. He had a quiet call, "sik sik"; and that is his Eskimo name. He was curious about my presence but not unduly alarmed. After inspecting me he went to work with a great burst of energy collecting roots and plants for his den under the hummock where I sat. This arctic ground squirrel is a true hibernator, and his winters are long. In June, when the Muries first arrived, the valley of the Sheenjek was still brown. Summer came in a great rush, July being the month when the bloom of the flowers was at the peak. By mid-August Summer was gone and Fall had set in. Even the first part of August showed fresh snow on the mountains. The arctic ground squirrel had his job cut out for him if he was to finish all his household tasks before freezing weather set in.

This busy animal that ran to and fro at my feet is important in the ecology of the Brooks Range. The grizzly bear digs into hummocks looking for him. The red fox, the lynx, and the wolverine are heavily dependent on him. The golden eagles, whose nest I saw on a cliff some miles east of camp, also hunt the arctic ground squirrel. Gyrfalcons and hawks join the chase. The arctic ground squirrel is essential in the food chain of the Sheenjek.

The next friend to appear was the willow ptarmigan. This bird, which mates in May and nests by the first of June, was quite silent in July and August. The white body feathers had been molted and the birds now wore the brown plumage of summer. This color blends perfectly with the willow, dwarf birch, and spruce boughs where the nests are cleverly hidden. The eggs have the same brown-splotched appearance; and the downies are so perfectly camouflaged they are almost impossible to see. The bird that approached me this morning was a male. He kept at a respectable distance, feeding on bearberries. Once he was startled and fled. It was a short, swift flight with a low trajectory; and though I saw where he landed I could not, for the life of me, see him.

The ptarmigan, like the ground squirrel, is important in the Sheenjek's food chain. Man, of course, finds this bird a delicious dish. The red fox hunts its eggs and its young. So do the ground squirrels. The golden eagle, marsh hawks, short-eared owls, and goshawks pursue the ptarmigan. So do the wolf and the wolverine. Every predator seems to rely on this bird for a part of its diet. And its feathers are important too. They are used by many birds, particularly the tree sparrows and white-crowned sparrows, to line their nests.

Last Lake, which was below me, suddenly seemed to come alive with birds. Cliff swallows hurried by; Brewer's blackbirds set up a chatter; some gray-cheeked thrushes were calling. An old squaw duck came gliding in. A pin-tailed duck with a young brood cruised a marshy point looking for food. Two Pacific loons—whose calls we were to hear infrequently—came out of some reeds, heading quickly for the middle of the lake. A number of lesser yellowlegs and numerous sandpipers—common shore birds in this region—combed the shores of Last Lake, looking for food. But the most frenzied activity was by the short-billed gulls. Two of them had a nest somewhere in the marsh by the lake. We were to see one large young one before we left. This day it was not in view. One of the gulls sat on the high stub of an ancient spruce, guarding the lake. I decided to walk over and inspect the site. I had no sooner started along the shore of the lake then several lesser yellowlegs flew from spruce to spruce, sounding the alarm with their ear-splitting cry—"whew, whew, whew, whew." But the short-billed gull needed no notice of my coming. I was still fifty yards from its perch when it dived on me. I kept going, and it dived again and again. I held my hands over my face as I splashed through the marshy stand of sedges and willows. Once more the gull dived, this time hitting my hat. I ignominiously retreated, taking as my excuse the antics of a female mallard, who feverishly scattered her young ones into the marshes and scuttled toward the middle of the lake showing a "broken wing."

I resumed my seat under the white spruce and noted that I was not the only intruder whom the short-billed gull resented. Out of the deep stillness of the Sheenjek came the clear, metallic croak of the raven—a friendly sound in the Arctic, where most voices are muted. I looked up to see two circling. The short-billed gull left like a fighter plane after bombers, chasing the ravens and diving on them from above. The gull resumed its vigil. The loons, which had been cruising Last Lake, got close to the shore where the nest of the gulls was located. Down came the gull over their heads, screaming and scolding. Again and again during our stay at Last Lake the short-billed gull stayed on guard, driving off any of our party that ventured close and chasing golden eagles and goshawks with a vengeance I had never seen.

I love fishing in the Arctic. There were many tributaries of the Sheenjek below camp—streams that drained Last Lake and the marshy ponds that lay below it. Some of these were deep sluices showing black bottoms from the sphagnum moss that flourishes in this valley. These fresh-water streams ended in a rather extensive piece of overflow ice that occupied perhaps ten acres or more. This overflow ice is formed by the pressure of water against the ice that forms in the stream bed. When the pressure is great, the water breaks through the ice and flows over it. It in turn is frozen. The process is repeated until many layers are formed, creating a body of ice six feet or more deep and many acres in size that lasts all summer.

Above the overflow ice were large holes in the deep, still water where I fished with flies. An old friend, the robin, hopped furtively in a stand of spruce. It was no longer the gay, spirited bird I had known farther south. But when I turned my back it burst forth with its old, familiar song. An Alaska jay flew up and scouted me, filled with curiosity. But in this arctic domain they are not the "camp robbers" I had expected them to be. They, too, seemed shy and furtive.

I was whipping my line preparatory to the first cast upstream when a muskrat came up from some pocket on the side of the stream and, seeing me, dived with a splash. These animals that are very much in evidence when the ice goes out and the mating season is on are inconspicuous as July advances. Their secretiveness must be rewarded, for they are sought after by all the birds of prey; and the wolf and the fox find them a delicacy.

I whipped the first piece of open water above the overflow ice without reward. My first cast in the next pool produced a slight swirl that would have gone unnoticed had not my eyes been glued on the spot. I set the hook and brought to net a fourteen-inch grayling. It did not show the fight our rainbow trout give. There was no standing on its tail, no shaking of its head. It went down like a pike and tried to stay there. I was to be rewarded over and again with grayling, striking a wet fly. Bob Krear, a member of the Murie party, knew these fish well and was adept at catching them. He explained that one of their mainstays was the beetle larvae. These waters hatch great quantities of caddis flies; and the pools I saw were rich with nymphs that I was not able to catalogue.

These grayling, which run up to three pounds or more, are not prepossessing. Their small heads and broad-beamed bodies make them seem a bit awkward compared with our streamlined rainbow. But whatever they lack in grace they make up in food. Their flesh is white and their thick steaks cook up into a sweeter and more delicious dish than any trout I have sampled. Bob Krear and I cleaned the grayling by Last Lake, throwing the offal into the shallow water. The short-billed gulls that had attacked me so relentlessly quickly appeared to enjoy the feast. They brought with them their lone offspring, who still was awkward and clumsy; and it was gray, not white like its parents. But it had its parents' aggressive instincts. A pin-tailed duck flew in to examine the shore line and was immediately attacked by the youngster.

It is said there are other fish in the Sheenjek—a word meaning "dog salmon" in the Kutchin Indian language. But I saw no salmon, nor did I see any lake trout, pickerel, or whitefish that have been reputed there. My only reward were the grayling, and they were enough to satisfy any fisherman.

We discovered on one of our exploratory hikes some pools that lie on one of the low knolls that dot this area. The pools, which drain to the river only when the rains come, are deep in the shade of white spruce, which generally forms an open forest but here had grown into a thick stand. Willow—a browse that caribou and moose enjoy in winter—was mixed with the spruce; and there were some stands of dwarf birch. Some of the spruce was hung with beardlike lichens, giving them almost a patriarchial appearance. Others were decorated with crustose lichens that grew like scales on the limbs—some red, some yellow, some gray. The ground around the pools was spongy and soft and covered with a thick mat of mosses. The mountain avens was in bloom, adding streaks of creamy white to the dark green. A dark blue saxifrage was mostly hidden. A tall lousewort—bright blue— showed its tiny heads. A small black berry, known as the crowberry, made a carpet. The arctic poppies were brilliant. Bush cinquefoil added a touch of gaiety. White, yellow, and gray lichens gave life and zest to the leaf litter; and the lovely, delicate, tiny bluebell flower was almost hidden from view. But what caught my eye was a moss I had never seen before, one which George Schaller, also in the Murie party, assured me was scarce. George gave me its technical name, *Splachnum luteum*. It has stems almost eight inches high, topped by small yellow umbrellas or hats. This moss has become so specialized that it can survive only on the dung of moose, an article in abundance around these pools.

It was difficult to express my feelings as I stood beside these dark quiet pools, shaded by spruce. They were so beautiful, so exquisite, that they were unreal. They seemed withdrawn from this earth, though a glorious part of it. The day had been cloudy; now the sun came out, brightening the dark waters. The black of their bottoms showed various tints of green. The delicate colors along the shore added life and zest. Here were pools never touched by man—unspoiled, uncontaminated except perhaps by the awful fall-out from the atomic bombs that is slowly poisoning the whole earth. Here was life in perfect ecological balance. A moose had stopped here to drink. Some water beetles skimmed the surface. Nothing else had seemed to invade this sanctuary.

It was indeed a temple in the glades. Never, I believe, had God worked more wondrously than in the creation of this beautiful, delicate alcove in the remoteness of the Sheenjek Valley.

These white-spruce forests are interesting to explore. They never grow above 3000 feet and their northernmost limit is just short of 69° N. In moist places they sometimes form thick stands. But they usually appear as long fingers, stretching northward up the Sheenjek Valley. They are a small tree with branches that cover the trunk. The branches are short, giving the tree a slim appearance, and the tip is peaked. Their average height is fifteen or twenty feet; and a foot or so from the ground they are usually not more than seven inches in diameter. There are some, however, that are nearly eighteen inches through. The Murie expedition found that it takes over thirty years for a white spruce in the Brooks Range to reach five feet and 100 years to reach twenty feet. The oldest white spruce they found was nearly 300 years old.

These white spruce are slowly reclaiming the Arctic. Their scarcity is due, it is thought, not to unfavorable environment but to the fact that they could take hold only after the ice sheets had receded. Since then the migration of the white spruce northward has never ceased.

But except for the soil hummocks where the white spruce grows, most of this Sheenjek Valley country is tundra. In lowland meadows are small islands a foot or so high. The land they enclose is called a polygon, a wet area where mosses, sedges, rushes, and prostrate willow grow. A horsetail—perennial aquatic —flourishes there, as does the wild cranberry. This swampy land surrounds Last Lake. One sloshes through it as he does in any marsh. The more typical tundra is a few feet higher. It is marked

by tussocks formed from a variety of vegetation. Most conspicuous is a cotton grass, sometimes known as hare's-tail. In
June this cotton grass is in bloom, showing hundreds of acres with
a bluish-gray cast. Mosses and lichens grow thick on these
tussocks. A bog rosemary with lovely pink blossoms adorns them.
Bog bilberries (smaller than blueberries and not good for eating)
flourish there. Bearberries with white flowers make a mat. A
dwarf and prostrate rhododendron decorates many tussocks. A
dwarf trailing willow possesses much of this high ground in the
bogs. A vigorous species of the grass of parnassus grows here,
mixed with a purple lousewort, violet butterwort, violet-purple
milk vetch, a low, greenish bunchflower, a white false asphodel.

The tussocks are from a few inches to a foot or two broad.
They are like tall mushrooms with grassy heads. They are not
steady underfoot, sinking and sometimes swaying. Mardy Murie
said that one who walked them had to be limp like a rag doll.
A hike through the tussock meadows is more strenuous than
climbing. One is continuously on edge to keep his balance, for a
misstep sends him down into deep slush. The result is that a
hiker tends to put on speed, barely touching one tussock and
practically jumping to the next. A day of walking a tussock
meadow is exhausting. Horses would flounder hopelessly. In
the summer this is country only for men with packs. I had seen
this tundra on an earlier trip stretching from the north side of
the Brooks Range to the Arctic Ocean. That tundra, though
differing in botanical detail from the tundra of the Sheenjek,
has the same general appearance. It is in the main a dwarf-shrub
heath marked by tussocks, and it runs for miles and miles. There
is a dreary monotony in its northern expanse. But here on the
Sheenjek it is a colorful community broken by knolls where

willow, alder, and birch form thickets, by the long fingers of spruce reaching north, and by the backdrop of rounded mountains covered with a soft nap of lichen and moss heath.

One day we hiked far up the Sheenjek, resting frequently on the dry hummocks where the white spruce grow. Usually the Sheenjek is crystal-clear; but the day of our hike was after a storm. So the river was muddy from drainage. Above Last Lake the Sheenjek breaks up into many small streams. The riffles were shallow; the gravel beds highly polished. Small sand bars had built up from favorable currents, and the islands between the fingers of the river were thick with willow. These stands of willow along the river are a favorite habitat of moose. There were many fresh tracks, but we saw none of the animals. Wolves travel this river bed in their hunt for game. The wolf signs —especially the scat—were fresh and numerous this day. Olaus found one track where a front paw measured 6 inches by 5.1 inches. I was to see wolves later, but we saw none on this hike. Red fox also follow the river bed, and while we found their tracks we did not see them. But I heard one barking far off to the west in some willow. We looked at every mud bar for signs of the grizzly bear, but found none. One of our great rewards this day was the low, lush blueberries that grow in splendor on the east bank. Hundreds of acres were in full fruit. The berries were ripe, and they were the sweetest we have known. We picked several pints and ate many for lunch. Then we lay on our backs in these stands of blueberries and took a nap to the soft music of the purling Sheenjek.

The day was bright. The storm that brought us rain left six inches or so of snow on the mountains. These 8000-foot ridges glistened with their white mantles and seemed cool and inviting.

No tree broke the soft flow of their lines, and cloud shadows changed their moods and our fantasies.

A turbulent tributary that comes into the Sheenjek about three miles north has white spruce growing thick along it. A few stray cottonwoods are to be found, and poplars flourish there. Beaver frequent the Sheenjek Valley, and some of them had been fresh at work cutting these poplars. These woods were thickly carpeted with moss—rich in color, springy underfoot. Some of it reminded me of the star moss that grows high in the Cascades and Wallowas. One type was a bright green. When we came to higher ground, we found a bright-yellow moss that made a deep carpet on the wilderness floor. And choicest of all was a gray lichen (endemic in Alaska) that Mercedes, my wife, and Mardy collected for its decorative effect on women's hats.

Not far up this tributary we found two large spruce poles standing upright in the ground, spanned by a third one. This was a cache for food made by prospectors, who designed it years ago to keep their supplies safe from animals.

This was ancient land of the Athabaskan Indians, composed of eight tribes making up the Kutchin nation. Their domain extended over the Brooks Range to the Arctic Ocean. Occasionally they fought the Eskimos. But they were essentially hunters and fishermen who settled on the Yukon and the larger rivers that feed it. Probably only a few frequented the Sheenjek, at least in its upper reaches. Things changed when the gold rush started. Prospectors came into the Sheenjek Valley. Before then, in 1847, the Hudson's Bay Company established a post at Fort Yukon and the fur trade began. The Indians accommodated the fur traders; even Eskimos crossed the Brooks Range and came down the Sheenjek, bringing furs to the trading post. Some of the Eskimos stayed, establishing villages. But since the 1920s little hunting or trapping has been done here. A few Indians still make excursions into the Brooks Range from the Yukon flats, looking mainly for wolves, on which there has been a $50 bounty; but not many of them make the effort. They are mostly congregated at Fort Yukon, 150 miles to the south and in Arctic Village, nearly 50 miles to the southwest of our camp. Some white men have come into the Sheenjek, but they have been few and far between. The Sheenjek since the 1920s has known only its primeval quiet and stillness. Life has gone on undisturbed by men. No food chains have been broken by the introduction of civilization. There is no more thrilling place to observe life in complete ecological balance than in this valley on the south slopes of the Brooks Range.

The spread of the tree line far into the Brooks Range has some relation to the temperature range. This relationship has been put by some students into a formula which suggests that if the mean temperature for the coldest month of the year is -14°F., the mean for the warmest month must be 50°F. If the mean for the coldest month is -40°F., the mean for the warmest month must reach 55.4°F. The requirements of this formula can be satisfied on the southern slopes of the Brooks Range.

The Summers on the Sheenjek are mostly sunny and warm, the July daytime average being about 61°F. At night the temperature drops to 40°F. and sometimes lower. While the summer days are in the main bright, clouds often drift in by midday. And July and August are the months of the year when there is the heaviest precipitation. We knew several all-rain days, the storms coming mostly from the south and southeast. But the precipitation on these south slopes of the Brooks Range is so slight that but for the arctic conditions this would be semidesert.

The total precipitation over the period of a quarter century averages slightly under seven inches a year, which is only a bit more than half of that of Wyoming's high plateau. The yearly snowfall is less than four feet on the average. But the winters are long and cold, the average January temperature being -21 °F. Summers are short in the Arctic. Early June flowerings produce seeds by July first. Early in August most arctic plants have completed the cycle and entered the seed phase. Even while the seeds are maturing, new leaf and flower buds develop near the surface of the soil, ready for next season's growth. Most of the seeds of these arctic plants are light and specially adapted for transportation by wind. A high percentage of plants depend, indeed, on the high velocity of arctic winds for their spread and migration. This early flowering that comes with such a rush is aided by the fact that the microclimate at which the plants live is warmer than ordinary temperature readings would reveal. For the temperature just under the soil surface may be as much as 40 °F. higher than the air temperature. So there may be enough warmth for photosynthesis to take place in the earth, though the air temperature indicates freezing.

But under the soil is permafrost, which conditions much of the life of the arctic. It lies about fourteen inches beneath the surface in the Sheenjek Valley. This permafrost acts as an impervious layer which prevents normal drainage. Rainfall that would be absorbed by the earth under normal conditions, producing no runoff, has startling effects in the Sheenjek. A half inch of rain or less will raise the level of Last Lake a foot or more, since the water runs off permafrost as it would off concrete. One morning after an all-night rain we found a new creek running by our camp.

These arctic soils are quite acid, due to poor drainage and

poor aeration; and they are deficient in nitrogen, because organic decay by bacterial action is very slow.

The thin soil and short growing period emphasize how perishable the arctic wilderness is. Overgrazing would cause great tragedy here. Lichens, on which caribou depend so heavily, would take a century to restore. This arctic wilderness is truly fragile. Never can it survive the full impact of civilization.

The Eskimos have graphic names for these summer months:
<pre>
May——month-of-fawning
June——egg-month
July——mosquito-month
August——berry-month
</pre>
July ran true to the Eskimo experience.

I had heard horrible stories of the mosquitoes of Alaska and went prepared with head nets. But I never used them. There are mosquitoes—many of them. Even after a frost—one of which we experienced—new crops of mosquitoes are born. They swarm up out of the marshland and tundra. They are not too bothersome when the wind blows. Once it dies down they rise from the ground on every step; and they are always present where the stands of spruce or poplar are thick. But the use of modern mosquito "dope" keeps them off the skin and hands. They still envelop the head and shoulders like a cloud, following one everywhere. But one gets accustomed to this—except when he eats. Then he must be in a tent to avoid getting a mouthful of mosquitoes. A tent with a floor and zipper flap can be made mosquitoproof with the help of a spray. At night the greater worry for one raised in a temperate zone is not the mosquito but the light. In July the sun sets over the Sheenjek Valley about midnight and rises an hour or two later. This means it sinks below the limestone peaks to the west, travels only a short arc, and rises. We are accustomed to darkness for deep sleep and the unraveling of cares. The newcomer misses night in the Arctic. But there are special rewards. Cloud effects, sunsets, the long afterglow, and the sunrise produce a riot of colors that even Arizona does not know.

There are lemmings and voles in this arctic region. These rodents—along with snowshoe hares and arctic ground squirrels —support an aristocracy of clever predators that include the fox, the lynx, and the arctic weasel. They are most active in the Summer, collecting and storing roots and grass for their winter needs. Olaus and George were busy trapping them by day and preparing the specimens by night. I followed them as they ran their trap lines, learning much about these animals that a casual visitor to the northland would never know. These tiny mouselike animals live at various elevations in the Brooks Range. Some of them possess networks of runways extending from tussock to tussock in the wet land around Last Lake. There are ponds, higher in the mountains, where they are also found. Some types of voles are found several thousand feet above the Sheenjek with their runways built through carpets of moss and through bare rocky outcrops. They seem never to be found on high, dry slopes. Their preference is for damp edges of lakes and swamps. And when the waters rise and their runways are flooded, they merely retreat temporarily to higher, drier ground.

The lemmings and voles travel cycles of life with periods when the population reaches crash proportions and times when it is at low ebb. The low point for lemmings had been reached this Summer, for they were not much in evidence. Lowell

Sumner and John Christian have shown that once these animals build to a high population level and then come into a period of food scarcity, they are subject to tremendous emotional stress. This stress leads to an exhaustion of the adreno-pituitary system. The effect on voles and lemmings is similar to the effect of stress on man. These rodents develop inflammation or ulceration of the digestive tract and a permanent metabolic derangement that directly or indirectly causes death. In lemmings this tension becomes so great that it leads to mass migration. This migration is not an orderly, methodical one, like settlers looking for new homes. It is a panicky outburst which amounts to mass suicide. The lemmings go on and on, stopped not even by rivers, lakes, or the ocean where they are destroyed.

There are Dall sheep in the Brooks Range; but they come down into the Sheenjek only in winter. George Schaller scouted the high slopes and found them in alpine meadows protected both above and below by talus slopes.

There are grizzly bear in these mountains, and their tracks and scat were evident on every trip. I also saw many places where they had dug for roots or for squirrels, and some where they had bedded down. But I never came across one, nor did I even see one from a distance. One charged to within thirty feet of George Schaller; another got even closer to Bob Krear on a charge that came to a sudden, grinding stop when Bob thought the end was near. These grizzlies—inherently shy—have very poor eyesight. Even at a hundred feet a man probably looks much like a caribou. The grizzly may have to come much closer to pick up the scent. When he does, he usually will run unless cornered or hurt. The scent of man is the signal of danger. The grizzly gets this message intuitively, for the sight or even the odor of a man is an experience that would come to a grizzly in the Sheenjek only once in a lifetime.

There are many caribou in the Sheenjek, the total number in the herd perhaps reaching 40,000. The caribou are the only members of the deer family where both sexes have antlers. Their summer coat is dark; their winter fur is a light tan. In the early Summer they move west. By August first they move east. These migrations are on a broad front of forty or fifty miles, not many caribou being in one group. I had seen small groups feeding around Last Lake. But they seldom stood still; they were a restless, nervous lot, seeming always to be on the move. One night an estimated 2000 caribou crossed the Sheenjek not far above our camp. Their feet pounding in the gravel sounded, as Mardy put it, like "a freight train roaring through the valley."

One day I hiked to a pass that marks the divide between the Sheenjek and the Coleen drainage. At the pass I climbed the southern slopes, looking for flowers. As I rested on a limestone outcropping, a herd of forty caribou crossed below me. They were headed east. Up ahead was a bull with head bowed under the great weight of his antlers. Lesser bulls followed. Then came the cows and the calves. Yearlings raced alongside. But every other animal followed in line, stepping in practically the same tracks as the one ahead of him. Their brown summer hair was prominent, though some had dark only along their backs. By Fall a light brown would take the place of the dark color, for the whole herd and the older bulls would have strikingly white necks. This day the caribou were traveling so fast that the calves had difficulty keeping up.

These restless animals depend on lichens, grasses, and sedges in the Winter; on willow and birch, grasses and sedges in the Summer. This day they were driven by some great force that made this migration an integrated community effort.

This country to the east of Last Lake was good hiking terrain. Above the tundra were the knolls, thick with stands of dwarf willow and birch, which by late August turn red and yellow. The moss makes thick, moist carpets in these thickets. The crowberry and bog bilberry flourish there. Here I found the Labrador tea in bloom—a species similar to that I once found along the northern slopes that face the Arctic Ocean. On the open slopes of these knolls mountain avens and cassiope left streaks of creamy white. Alpine hedysarum added touches of violet; lousewort and arnica showed yellow; knotweed was bright pink; the arctic lupine added bright blue; and the arctic poppy showed gold. A mosslike silene, known as cushion pink, showed pink and rose flowers growing on almost stemless stocks. A minute larch-leaf sandwort also flourished here. But what caught the eye on these knolls and the slopes above them was the rhododendron. Some call this plant an azalea, but its name is *Rhododendron lapponicum*. It virtually blankets the lower hillsides of the Sheenjek Valley, turning them cerise, and the air is saturated with the fragrance of its delicate blossoms. To one who has seen the south slopes of the Brooks Range in July, the sight and smell of the rhododendron are never forgotten.

The slopes above these knolls are drier. But they too are green with a nap of sedges, low shrubs, and lichens. White heather is everywhere. Anemones grow here in white patches. Yellow cinquefoil nod gracefully in the wind. A purple locoweed is found here, and occasionally a yellow saxifrage. The low evergreen shrub—kinnikinnick—hugs the ground. So does a dwarf, rose-pink phlox. The fairy forget-me-not, almost destitute of stems, shows cerulean blue. Camass lilies grow in clumps.

All life on these slopes is prostrate. I came across prostrate willow and birch that were using the south face of upturned rocks as a trellis where they got added heat from the sun. I stopped to examine their roots and found them running at length horizontally under the surface to avoid the permafrost. In a ravine fed by springs or on a low spot where drainage is poor, meadow conditions exist even high in the Brooks Range. Then the mosses and lichens are on brilliant display. Shooting stars brighten wet spots. Purple monkshood and purple gentians grow against rich green banks. Here, too, are dainty alpine buttercups and the familiar Jacob's ladder, two feet higher and showing dark-blue flowers.

The higher one goes, the scarcer the vegetation. When the talus slopes are reached, the lichens are the only plants that flourish; they spot the rocks red and black and cover the ground in white or yellow patches. An occasional prostrate willow has taken hold in the rocks. Mats of the rosaceae cling stubbornly to thin soil, kept company by the dwarf evergreen cassiope that John Muir loved so much.

One day, while hiking the ridge to the east of camp, I had left the last fingers of white spruce and came to an open, exposed promontory. I heard a deep-throated roar underground. Some great subterranean creek was rushing through the porous lime-stone that forms these mountains. The wind blew a gale. It was cold and piercing and brought squalls of rain. This was only the third of August, but Fall had arrived. Not many days distant Keith Harrington from Fort Yukon would drop through low clouds in his Cessna plane to take us out.

Today the two short-billed gulls with their grayish youngster had taken off, heading for the south. Their departure made the camp seem lonely. Now that I was high above Last Lake, the feeling of loneliness and isolation mounted. As I turned to view the valley at my feet, it seemed that I was remote from our civilization, looking down on this earth from an aperture in the sky. There was not a movement in the vast expanse below me. Suddenly a lone caribou came out of a stand of spruce and willow, moving hurriedly toward a pass that led eastward and nibbling at low shrubs as it went. Far below on the flats, where the river runs, a moose and a calf browsed peacefully. Below the caribou but still high above camp a wolf loped leisurely along. He, too, was headed for the pass. There are black wolves in these mountains, but this was a gray one. It was a magnificent specimen. I had seen wolves before both in this country and in Afghanistan and Persia. Wherever they roam they are considered dangerous. They are fast being removed from our national scene. The Brooks Range is probably their last refuge. But even here they are hunted, a $50 bounty being on them. Why should this be? Why should man be committed to destroy this magnificent animal? These were my thoughts as I watched the great, gray wolf lope gracefully across the slopes below me.

We have some things to learn from the wolf. When wolves circle each other, threatening and growling, the less aggressive one often turns his cheek. This is not a signal to the other one to move in for the kill. The wolf who turns his cheek asks for a truce, and though the snarling continues, the truce is always granted. Turning the other cheek, the wolf teaches us, is not abject surrender but an honorable way to prevent a fight and save the species. As Lorenz wrote in *King Solomon's Ring*, "A wolf has enlightened me: not so that your enemy may strike you again do you turn the other cheek toward him, but to make him unable to do it."

The wolf is a predator. Olaus Murie studied wolf scats collected in the Sheenjek and discovered that of forty-one samples there were thirty-eight that contained caribou. We found several kills around Last Lake. But how many wolves they fed we did not know. How many other predators, such as the red fox and the lynx, are maintained on caribou carrion left by wolves is also not known. But we have reason to think that the wolf is important to their survival.

The wolf, though fast and powerful, cannot outrun a healthy caribou. Apart from those he catches by surprise, he is dependent on cripples and on calves. Sheep also can elude him; and moose usually stand him off. The wolf does not decimate herds; he merely helps control their size, and in that way acts as a curb on the destructive overuse of the national range.

It may be necessary to control the wolf in the environment of ranges where cattle roam. But here in the Sheenjek the wolf is as much a part of the environment as the arctic ground squirrel, the ptarmigan, and the short-billed gulls. This is—and must forever remain—a roadless, primitive area where all food chains are unbroken, where the ancient ecological balance provided by nature is maintained. The wolf helps in that regard. He has, moreover, a charm that is wild and exciting. In this, our last great sanctuary, there should be a place for him. His very being puts life in new dimensions. The sight of a wolf loping across a hillside is as moving as a symphony.

The vast, open spaces of the arctic are special risks to grizzlies, moose, caribou, and wolves. Men with field glasses and high-powered rifles, hunting from planes, can well-nigh wipe them out. In this land of tundra, big game has few places to hide. That is another reason why this last American living wilderness must remain sacrosanct. This is the place for man turned scientist and explorer, poet and artist. Here he can experience a new reverence for life that is outside his own and yet a vital and joyous part of it.

CHAPTER II

PACIFIC BEACH

THE wildest, the most remote and, I think, the most picturesque beach area of our whole coast line lies under a pounding
surf along the Pacific Ocean in the State of Washington. It is
marked as Cape Alava on the north and the Quillayute River on
the south. It is a place of haunting beauty, of deep solitude.

Whenever I hike it, I go in from Lake Ozette, a large fresh-
water lake, and take the trail west to Cape Alava. It's a good trail,
about three and a half miles long, and passes through a thick

forest. Giant Sitka spruce with their powerful upward sweep dominate the trail. This is the tree the lumbermen like for its strength, lightness, and uniform texture. It is choice for sounding boards in pianos.

Western hemlock, a hundred feet or more high, with thick, flat branches help shut out the sun. Their needles lie in a flat spray; their branches bend down at the tips, giving them a weeping effect. Their shade is dense; and being dense, the shade serves a high purpose. Young hemlocks thrive there; seedlings of other species are shaded out. This lovely tree was long despised by loggers. Now it is one of the chief sources of rayon in this country and the most common base of those plastics that are made from wood cellulose. Happily, it grows fast enough to keep ahead of the demands of those who harvest it.

Now and then a western red cedar with its stringy, grayish-brown bark, drooping limbs, and lacy branches also reaches high to claim a piece of the sky. This is the canoe cedar that the Indians used extensively, not only for canoes but for twine, hats, ropes, nets, baskets, and shawls. It is today unexcelled for resistance to decay. It makes our choice shingles, racing shells, and cruisers.

Closer to the ocean are the Oregon alder, whose grayish-white bark is adorned with blackish splotches—the tree whose leaves on the underside flash silver in the wind. Like the birch and aspen, this tree brightens the woods, as every fisherman knows. It loves creeks and bays and bogs. It furnished the firewood for the people who settled this area. It is still the favorite. But it is a hardwood which lumbermen these days cut for an expanding furniture market.

These are the trees that unite to put a green canopy over this beach forest, a roof through which only occasional shafts of sunshine penetrate. Underneath is down timber so tangled and high that a horse can travel only with great difficulty. Logs ten feet or more in diameter are being reclaimed and turned to humus. This is an area of heavy precipitation—nearly twelve inches a month. Down logs are soon covered with thick moss and lichens.

In this wildwood are ferns shoulder high, salmonberries, nettles, blueberry elder (whose pithy stems make excellent flutes), and a shrub known as devil's club because of its sharp spines that tear the flesh and the big ball-like knot that grows at the base, where the roots spread out. The Indians valued this shrub for its medicinal and even magic qualities. They wore amulets of its wood, and they made an emetic from its bark which was administered with hot sea water.

Out of this almost impenetrable forest, Lars K. Ahlstrom early in the century made a clearing and built himself a home. He was a Swede who came in from the ocean after a shipwreck, saw the beach forest, and liked it. I met him on one trip and found him as refreshing as his accent. Now his ranch is in the Olympic Park. The buildings are drooping and will soon be reclaimed. Bracken and Oregon alder are taking hold in the fields where Ahlstrom once grew hay for his milk cows. The grass, blended with bright blue gentian, is knee-high. A black-tailed deer feeding in a pasture neatly cleared a fence on my approach. Only the memory of Ahlstrom's ranch would soon remain.

The trail drops off a dune of loose sand strewn with logs to a coarse-gravel beach, the site of an ancient Indian village. This is Cape Alava which was, until Alaska was added, the westernmost point in the United States. Offshore about a mile is Ozette Island, and beyond it a reef so dangerous to ships that the Umatilla Lightship stays there permanently. One night August

Slathar—woodsman and smoker of salmon *par excellence*—and I camped on the edge of this beach under an ancient spruce. A raging storm had driven a fleet of several dozen fishing boats to the lee of the island. The dim lights of their cabins bobbed like fireflies over the water. Beyond them a booming foghorn announced all through the bitter night that death and danger were present.

There is a creek that flows at Camp Alava, losing itself in the sands before it reaches the ocean. It is yellowish water, stained by hemlock and given that name by the local people. But hemlock water is usually sweet to the taste and healthful for man. One year, when Augie and I made the hike alone, this creek was running full. Another year, when seventy of us made the hike in protest to a plan to construct a road along the beach and despoil it, the creek was dry; even the spring from which it came was low. That year had been a very dry one. A region that averages 144 inches of rain a year had suffered a drought for three months. Usually this Olympic beach spouts a fresh-water stream every quarter mile or so. That year most of them had dried up. Usually the woods above the beaches are so moist that spruce and hemlock needles can be cleared away and fireplaces built almost anywhere. This year the forest was dry as a bone; the thick carpet of needles was like tinder; the fire hazard great. All fires had to be built on the beach.

This beach is one to walk at low tide. The coast line is a series of beaches, usually a quarter or a half mile long and guarded at each end by a headland, on a few of which the Coast Guard built lookouts during World War II. The points of these headlands cannot be passed at high tide. Then one must climb over them. They are only a few hundred feet high at most, but their pitch is steep; and some of them are thick with the salal bush, whose berries are dark purple and quite choice, the Indians making a drink out of them or drying the fruit for winter's use. But salal presents a thicket that is almost impassable.

On one of the first headlands south of Cape Alava is Wedding Rock, a dark-basalt cliff with broken rocks at its base. These rocks have served as a canvas for ancient artists. Here are lively petroglyphs carved on the rocks. Petroglyphs are common throughout America. Picture writing was not confined to any one tribe or group. It existed wherever there were cliffs for writing. Washington State, with its great basalt formations, is conspicuous for its petroglyphs. The ones at Wedding Rock are simple pictures of the killer whale, of Indian masks, and of men. Others seem to carry the mark of obscenity. Perhaps the Makahs to the north or the Quillayutes to the south carved them. No one seems to know.

Each headland presents a beach of distinction. Some have sand made from dark volcanic rock, and packed so hard that a deer leaves few tracks on it. Some beaches are filled with a whitish, loose sand that flows freely between the toes. Others have sand, too coarse for packing, that is streaked with pebbles. Some of this sand is so loose and heavy that half of every step is lost in a backward movement. A few are a millennium from hard-packed sand, being lined with boulders and ledges of rock that tides without number have yet to pulverize. Most beaches have logs strewn along them or piled high on their upper reaches. Some of them have fallen from the adjoining forest, worked loose by the angry tides that come with winter gales and bite ferociously into the land. Some logs have broken loose from booms pulled by tugs far out beyond the dangerous shoals. Logs that reach the beach in the winter have been rolled smooth by summer. Some giants have been piled so high by ferocious waves as to be dozens of feet beyond the reach of any high tide that comes in Summer.

Pieces of ships, wrecked on hidden reefs, are often added to the pile. Once Augie and I came across a fishing vessel quite intact and sitting upright in the sand, as if in a drydock for repairs. And it is on these Olympic beaches that one can find the prized Japanese glass balls that have broken away from the fishing nets they help float and drifted thousands of miles across the Pacific. I have found so many I had no room to carry them.

The force of winds and tides is often so great as to change completely the character of some beaches from one year to the next. On my first hike Augie and I stopped for lunch on a beach of hard sand where a clear, cold stream came tumbling out of the forest onto the white beach. An Oregon alder with mottled bark leaned out over the beach. We stopped in its shade. A one-masted steamer far offshore headed north. Dry chips of driftwood made a quick fire, and we propped a stick against a rock to hold our teapot over the flames. The beach was almost as hard as concrete, and this smooth sand extended even beyond the limits of low tide. This day the ebb tide washed the shore softly and quietly. A spotted sandpiper, feeding near the shore, suddenly jumped into the air after an insect sailing by. The leaning alder, hard sand, the crackling fire, and gentle tide made an idyllic scene that I carried for years in my memory. My dream was to return to that spot, find an old spruce behind the beach for a camp site, and spend several days in the shade of the alder soaking up as much of the solitude as possible. Some years later the chance came. I hurriedly rounded the point marking the upper limits of my beach. What I saw made me disappointed. My leaning alder had disappeared. So had the hard-packed sand. The tree and the finely ground sand had gone out in some wild storm. Thousands upon thousands of tons of gravel had been deposited in their place. All that was left of the idyllic scene was my bright memory of it.

The storms that have pounded these shores have sent many ships and sailors to watery graves. Two disasters are memorialized. One is just above Cedar Creek, where I usually camp the first day out of Cape Alava. It is a difficult monument to find, for its site is heavily overgrown with ferns and salal bush. It was erected to commemorate a Swedish ship and eighteen crew members who perished in a storm on January 2, 1903. Their names were carved on this pointed granite shaft, and under them the names of the two survivors who erected the monument. The names are now indistinct, as wind, rain, and frost have slowly erased them. Below Cape Johnson—about midway to Lapush on the second day's hike—is the Chilean Memorial Monument, a copper plaque on a granite shaft commemorating a Chilean freighter lost in the treacherous waters off Cape Johnson. The monument was quite intact when I first saw it. But when seventy of us came through, the shaft was down and someone, who apparently came by boat, had made off with the copper plate.

When the winds are high and the days dark, the beach is forbidding. Every headland looms in ghostly fashion through the mist. The tops of the alder and spruce are lost to sight. The air is full of spray. The logs that cram the upper parts of the beach move with the waves that reach them. And when they move, the whole coast line seems animated. Great waves break on every headland, making passage treacherous. The beach at these times is no place for man. Then it's better to follow the elk inland and find shelter from the storm's fury in the thick woods.

On a summer's day this wilderness beach is a bit of paradise.

The stars are bright at night; and if one has chosen his time wisely, he will find the moon shining over waters that gently touch the beaches. By morning, fog that is thick and low has swallowed the entire coast line. A person disappears from view at camp's edge or walks as a ghostly figure. Rocks and islands that lie offshore come and go in the swirling mist. The logs piled high along the shore assume strange and grotesque forms. Everything seems out of focus. As the ceiling moves upward, patches of fog still blur the vision, making offshore islands disappear and then come magically back into view. The place seems unreal—a part of some far-off place of mystery. The Hole in the Rock is at these times the most fascinating of all. It lies near the take-out point of the hike, above the Quillayute River near the northern edge of Rialto Beach. A huge granite cliff forms a shoulder that protrudes into the Pacific, blocking passage on foot. Wind and sand have worn a hole through it, a large arching cave that finally broke the barricade. Hard, glistening sand packs the beach. The cliffs rise high behind it. In the fog this opening in the rock is a keyhole to the supernal land where rolling mists form weird shapes and only the sound of surf is familiar to man.

The sun is always high when the fog has gone. Some days a fresh wind blows from the northwest. At other times there is no breath of air to make the alder leaves glisten. At these times I like to put my pack under a spruce and lie in the grass above the beach, watching the waves come in from Asia. When the wind is high there is always a booming sound from the nearby point. When the air is breathless, the waves are soft and gentle and faraway. Then the quiet of the bench above the beach is so deep I have heard the pods of the brome grass breaking—a faint, crackling sound that the ear can hear only when there is deep quiet. Time passes quickly in these idle hours of dreaming. I dream of far-off peoples who share the Pacific with us. I think of time and the universe and the unseen forces that have made the earth of which we are a part. I realize how small and minute man is in the cosmic scheme. Yet how bold and aggressive and dangerous he has become. Now he has unlocked the secrets and can destroy and sterilize for eons the good earth from which we all came. Earth, the hard sand below me, the waves that make it, the alder and spruce above me, the ferns and brome grass that envelop me—all this seems newly precious, almost sacred. We look to the heavens for help and uplift, but it is to the earth we are chained; it is from the earth that we must find our sustenance; it is on the earth that we must find solutions to the problems that promise to destroy all life here.

I like to lose myself in the solitude of this beach—the solitude that no automobile can puncture. It is then I think of a passage in Darwin's *Autobiography*:

". . . if I had to live my life again, I would have made a rule to read some poetry and listen to some music at least once every week; for perhaps the parts of my brain now atrophied would thus have been kept active through use. The loss of these tastes is a loss of happiness, and may possibly be injurious to the intellect, and more probably to the moral character, by enfeebling the emotional part of our nature."

I would add, that to be whole and harmonious, man must also know the music of the beaches and the woods. He must find the thing of which he is only an infinitesimal part and nurture it and love it, if he is to live.

These quiet hours of bright summer days are in a way the most rewarding that the beach has to offer. At low tide some of the flat lava ledges that extend a hundred yards or so to the sea show exciting produce. There is the seaweed known as sea sac or popweed, whose pods break with a crackling sound underfoot. Pompon kelp sends its tough streamers up from watery crevices. The split whip wrack floats its blades on the waves. Specimens of the sea girdle—the brown algae from which iodine is made—are scattered on the rocks. Pieces of the brown sieve, host to many seaweed tenants, are flat in placid pools. The fir-needle seaweed, used in Japan as a food, covers some of the rocks. And the red rock crust covers many of the rocks with a stony encrustation and, like other seaweeds, produces a variety of food for animals.

There are rivulets in these lava ledges where the waves have worn channels. Holes have also been worn there, some as big as a barrel. Gravel caught in a depression whirls and whirls under the force of the tides. Gradually the spinning gravel wears a deep hole in the black basalt. High tides fill these holes with water and with life.

This western shore of ours, thanks to abundant supplies of plankton in the water, is rich in marine life. The deep offshore waters and the wind play major roles in producing the plankton. The runoff waters from the land bring fertilizers which feed the plankton, once the sunlight starts. The growth is great until the fertilizers are used up. Then the plankton colonies die out, their constituent elements sinking to the dark, deep layers of the sea. Winds from the northwest push the coastal waters southward and outward. The reaction comes in the form of vertical currents from the depths. These upwellings bring up the fertilizers—phosphates, silicates, and nitrates. Then the colonies of plankton multiply fast. That is why the waters off this coast, unlike many others, have a high standard of fertility during the Spring and Summer.

That is the reason marine biologists love this area. We saw some of the marine fauna. One was the sand flea, which appeared in some coves by the thousands. They are one of the many scavengers that keep the edge of the sea clean. We usually saw them feasting on decaying seaweed. Many sand dollars, dark purple to black, were partly buried in the sand at low tide. They, too, scour the sand for bits of food.

The rocks were covered with acorn barnacles, small and grayish. Some rocks had colonies of them so thick the rock surface was completely covered. These small crustaceans open their hinged mouths in high tide and sweep the water with their appendages, searching for food. In the tide pools carved in the rocks there were many hermit crabs with bright red antennae, sometimes called clowns for the way they rush around. In one water-filled hollow were a large red starfish, several brown snails, some small red sponges, a few sea spiders, and big roundworms.

Sea urchins, whose name derives from a Latin word meaning hedgehog and who are related to the starfish, were also in these pools. They bristled with spines. These deep-sea denizens are one of our oldest forms of life. Fossil specimens going back 400 million years have been found. They were once used like oysters and clams for food—they can be found in some European and American markets to this day—and they are eagerly sought after by the crab and the sea otter. Once they were used by doctors to cure ulcers, tumors, scrofula, and kidney stones. The ones lying almost motionless before me were purplish in color. This purple urchin often uses its teeth and spines to grind away the rock to make the hole that catches the fresh tidewater.

In some of the tide pools I found greenish anemones—cylindrical shaped with long tentacles slowly waving. The green color is produced by symbiotic green algae which actually live in the tissues of the animal. This delicate flower of the sea can exist for long periods without food; then it seems to live on itself, shrinking in size as its fast continues. But even in the tidal pools its sensitive tentacles comb the water for food. These anemones seem to take all substances that the tides bring in, even inert matter. They are voracious feeders. They are scavengers and have been known to swallow a clam. They also swallow crabs, and have such a fast digestive process that they shortly spew out the shells.

Another active scavenger is the beach hopper, always present in great numbers. They seem aimless in their movements, going every which way. They perform an important function. Every tide brings in some carcass. But for these scavengers the shore line might reek. The busy, active beach hoppers help keep the edges of the sea clean, the sands as tidy as a swept hearth, the waters fresh. It not only digs out the meat from shellfish and picks all bones clean, it also reduces to fiber the great lacy weeds that the tides leave behind.

Overhead were the greatest scavengers of all, the seagulls that reported early every morning and followed us all day long.

On a warm, soft day the harbor seals (which some call hair seals) are present. This water, which is 51° in summertime, is ideal for them. The rocks and islands offshore have bizarre shapes. One is like a cake—such, indeed, is its name. Others are like partially submerged submarines. Some are pointed shafts, adorned at the top by a lone spruce or two. Others look like remnants of ancient blockhouses. They are all covered with seals on a warm day. There are many stories about these seals. One concerns Wesley Smith, who died in 1938. He was a big man— six feet two and weighing 220 pounds. He had sandy hair and blue eyes. He was a homesteader at Lapush and taught school there for twenty-two years. For five years he carried the mail from Neah Bay (which is north of Cape Alava) to Lapush. Part of the time he went by canoe. Usually he went on foot, making the 40-odd miles in two days of hiking, carrying the mailbag on his shoulder. He carried no pack with him, though he slept out. He never drank tea or coffee, and his food for one trip was one huge, thick pancake, fried in a large pan. So he traveled light. He always carried an ocarina, which he would play while hiking the beach. On calm, quiet days the seals would leave their rocks to follow him. They brought up the rear, staying about a hundred feet from shore. Once he had a chorus of thirty seals almost at his heels.

The harbor seals were active on my trips. The night seventy of us camped at Sand Point, which is about three miles below Cape Alava, the water was fairly alive with them as they came close to shore, apparently puzzled over our arrival.

I have seen marten swimming near the shore, and once a companion of mine caught a young sea pigeon too weak to fly, a bird whose true name is the black petrel.

Raccoon tracks are always numerous on the Olympic beach. These animals come down to find shellfish—clams and crabs— just as we do. I have also seen many bear tracks in the sand, but the bears have eluded me. Wesley Smith had a real encounter. A cub was near the water's edge and the mother was in the spruce. Wesley Smith was in between. The she-bear charged him. He dropped his mailbag and ran toward the open sea. The bear stopped momentarily to maul the bag and then went after Smith. He got as far out as he could without swimming when the heavy surf, pounding on his back, brought him back to the bear. Once more he retreated; once more the surf carried him in.

And so it continued on and on, until the cub made for the woods. To this day the Indians at Lapush tell how one batch of letters from Smith's mailbag had teeth marks through them.

The elk are thick in the wilderness behind the beach. But they seldom come onto the sand. The deer are different. These are the black-tailed deer that seem to like seaweeds that the tides bring in. They mate in late Fall, and the main concentration of fawn births is in June. In the month of June—the peak of the fawning period—deermeat makes up 50 per cent or more of the diet of the coyotes which frequent this area. Bear is the fawn's next worst enemy. For the first two weeks the fawn is hidden by its mother and suckled at night. Then the fawn follows· its mother until it is weaned, in three to five months. Meanwhile doe and fawn travel together; when they are flushed, they break in different directions, the doe beating an obvious retreat to draw the predator away from her fawn.

The time to see these black-tailed deer is in early morning, when the fog is rising from the ocean.

I remember one such morning when Augie and I were alone. We broke camp shortly after five o'clock, and for the first half hour or so Augie, who took the lead, would disappear in billowing fog at a distance of a dozen paces. We picked our way carefully around the first headland. The rocks were slippery, the going treacherous, the pace slow. By the time we rounded this point the fog had risen above the treetops. Below us was a hard-sand beach shaped like a fishhook. We clambered down the tumbled pile of boulders and rested under a sheer cliff that bounds the north end of this beach. Sweet water trickled from a rock. A few alder leaned gracefully toward the ocean. But the fringe of trees bordering the beach was mostly spruce. It stood in thick groves along the edge of the forest. These spruce were shorter than the giants that grow inland. They were old—perhaps several hundred years old. They had lived in great adversity on the ocean's edge. They had felt through the decades the full force and power of the storms that break there. Unlike their brothers in the deep interior forests, they had trunks covered by numberless boughs, and their branches swept low to the ground. But what gave them grace and dignity was their wind-swept tops. Their crowns had been touched by every breeze that blew. The great blows from the south and west that come in the winter had shaped their crowns as the hands of a potter shape clay. Adversity had given them character and distinction. They had gained beauty and strength under the mighty forces that assaulted them.

Augie and I sat for perhaps a half hour lost in our thoughts; then I saw a movement in a stand of alders half way down the beach. In a second a doe stepped gingerly into view, her ears twitching. Sensing that all was well, she came down the bank onto the hard sand. Behind her came a spotted fawn not many weeks old. Mother and child stood as still as statues for a few moments and then headed toward the salt water's edge.

I had color film in my Contax, but to get a picture I had to move a dozen feet. That motion was enough to sound the alarm. The doe turned and faced me, her big ears up. The click of the camera frightened her; away she went, bounding toward the forest. She stopped at its edge to watch the fawn, who dropped flat on the beach and froze. I moved quickly into action. I took photos of it at fifty, thirty, twenty, ten feet. It did not move. It blended so perfectly with the sand, driftwood, and seaweed that I might well have passed it by. At ten feet I could see its heart beat. I moved to six feet, then to three. Still no movement of the fawn except for its heartbeat. Finally I reached out to caress it. Even when my hand touched the fawn the little one did not move. Its heart was pounding hard, but some instinct deeply ingrained and resting in influences that need no conscious act to command them held the fawn frozen to the ground. Only when I returned to the cliff where I had dropped my pack and waited silently several minutes did the fawn move. Then it trotted from the beach at some command of its mother.

When I first camped at Cedar Creek, the sloping beach that ran from majestic wind-swept spruce to the ocean was smooth and well packed. Here we once found sea shell mounds which were part of the midden, or debris, of an ancient Indian village. It was probably a summer village. At some of these sites sea shell middens go down six feet. They mark camps where the Indians saw sunsets and sunrises without number during years when the ocean was washing the coast line far out where only islands stand today. Now the surf has carried most of the sea shell midden away. When the large group of us made the hike, I discovered that Cedar Creek had been transformed. Mighty tides and storms had piled coarse gravel twenty feet high midway on the beach. In front, the beach was just as smooth and charming as before. Behind the high gravel bar was a narrow belt of flatland. Then came Cedar Creek, at this point quite deep, and beyond it the forest. Since the wind was high, we decided to build our fire on the lee side. That arrangement was convenient for all our purposes. A great Sitka spruce had fallen years ago over Cedar Creek and now made an ideal footbridge.

So we built our fires and cooked on the ocean side of Cedar Creek, and put our bedrolls under the great spruce trees in the forest.

I never sleep better than when I am under a tree, and of all the trees I choose the Sitka spruce first.

It provides an ideal place for a sleeping bag. Its roots are mammoth, running close to the surface of the ground and extending far and wide. The height of these trees (200 feet is quite common) and their towering size (a diameter of 10 feet is customary) must create special problems for them, as they grow mostly in wet, soggy country. The roots seem to strike up and out, not down, in a heroic effort to grip the earth and hold their mighty master in place. The spots between these outcropped roots are made to order for bedding down. In the Olympic area of the Pacific Northwest the needles, which bristle on all sides of the twig at right angles, make a thick carpet on the ground. Eight inches of Sitka spruce needles is common, and they are as good as most air mattresses.

My spruce was right on the edge of Cedar Creek and close to the footbridge. Sig Olson was on the other side of the footbridge under another spruce. I went to bed early, Sandy, our Shetland sheep dog, by my side. Jupiter showed near a crescent moon. Then I was sung to sleep by the pounding of the incoming tide.

Sometime in the night skunks invaded our kitchen, across Cedar Creek from our bedroom. Sandy started barking. He was beside himself when the dishes were knocked off a log. It was all I could do to keep him from crossing the log to tackle the skunks. The skunks became agitated and gave up their foraging. They raced across the log, seeking to escape into the forest before Sandy descended on them. When they reached the other side and started to turn left, I counted them in the bright moonlight. They were four in all, and they seemed to be in a great hurry. Sig Olson's bed lay right across their path and Sig was in it. I had seen Sig move and knew he was awake. But now he was motionless. The four skunks walked right across his bedroll, stepping gingerly, so it seemed to me. Then they were swallowed up in the darkness of the brush.

In the morning Sig and I were laughing about the episode.

"What did you do?" I asked.

"What did I do?" he rejoined. "I didn't even breathe for a couple of minutes."

I always leave this primitive beach reluctantly. The music of the ocean front seems to establish a rhythm in man. For hours and even days afterward I can almost hear the booming of the tides on the headlands and the sound of the wind in the giant spruce.

On my last trip I turned inland at Rialto Beach to reach the road that leads to civilization. I had not gone far when I met a party carrying signs. They were protesting the preservation of this ocean strip as a primitive area and urging instead the construction of a highway that would turn it into another Atlantic City or Coney Island. That action was to me the desecration of a place of beauty and wonderment. I did not argue with the pickets. But I did ask them if all wilderness trails had to be paved, if all mountain peaks had to have chair lifts, if no sanctuaries could be left.

"Do roads have to go everywhere? Can't we save one per cent of the woods for those who love wildness?"

CHAPTER III

MIDDLE FORK OF THE
SALMON

THE sixteen-foot rubber boat floated lazily in midstream. The water was so clear and calm I could see the reflection of a granite cliff that towered almost a mile above us. An otter swam noiselessly near shore. A kingfisher dived from an overhanging branch. Somewhere far up the canyon wall an eagle screeched. All else was quiet. Only by sighting a pine on the canyon wall could I tell we were drifting.

Ralph Smothers, my guide, and I drifted in silence. I was at the stern, sitting on the rounded edge of the rubber boat. I leaned against a three-foot stretch of canvas which Ralph had laced to upright aluminum tubing so as to protect passengers from spray. Ralph stood on the "deck" of the rubber boat—two wooden boxes, holding our groceries, that were placed midships. Ralph held a sweep in each hand—one fore and one aft. Each of these sweeps swung on a metal pivot, laced to the boat. They had three-foot blades that could be used to steer the boat or to propel it.

Soon a side current caught the boat and carried it at a brisk speed along the shore. Ralph, who is slight and wiry, moved the boat with deft side movements of the sweeps back to the center of the river, where we caught the main current. Now we drifted at about three miles an hour.

"Grouse Creek Rapids coming up," Ralph said. "We'll need the life jackets here."

We put them on as we rounded a corner of the canyon. Quickly a place that had been deep in solitude was filled with a roar. The rapids were immediately ahead of us.

Grouse Creek Rapids fall about eight feet in fifty yards. The river at this point passes over a ledge that is twelve feet wide and at one point is as sharp as a razor. Rubber boats have been cut to pieces here, when the pilot kept too far to the right. Ralph hit the slick of the falls near the center of the ledge and the boat slid over gracefully. Then it dived, the stern rising high in the air. The nose hit the bottom of the trough and the boat seemed almost to buckle, with its bow on one side of the trough, its stern on the other. Then it started up the big wave, called the rollback. The boat climbed this wall of water in a flash, and for a split second hung over it in mid-air. Then we nose-dived a second time, and the stern flipped so high it showed blue sky between its bottom and the river. We crashed into the bottom of the trough with a thud that sent gallons of water into spray. Ralph turned to me with a grin as the boat leveled off and bobbed like a cork along the minor riffles at the tail of the rapids. With quick side motions of the sweeps he brought the boat to shore to pick up Bob Sandberg and Mercedes, who had been photographing the run from below.

The Middle Fork of the Salmon River in Central Idaho is a fast, white-water river for all of its 130 miles. During the first forty miles it drops sixty feet to the mile. The rest of the way it drops sixteen feet to the mile. It has eleven main rapids in its 130-mile length, not to mention the many pieces of white water that present no special navigation problem. Each of the eleven rapids has its own special risks. In some the danger is from concealed rocks. In others, the position of rocks often makes it necessary to change the course of the boat in the midst of the white water. In some, the main risk is the rollback wave at the bottom of the big drop-off. In every rapids there is the risk of the boat's turning sidewise and being crushed by the rollback.

Though some boatmen use oars or paddles, sweeps are by far the best guarantee of a safe journey. Yet even sweeps present problems. The blade of the sweep can take only a small "bite" of white water. If it dips too far into white water, no man can hold it. If he tries, he'll be yanked into the river. Ralph saw that happen once on Rubber Rapids, a falls so named for the bouncing one gets in a long series of big waves that stretch out a hundred yards or more. The boat behind Ralph entered Rubber Rapids properly and rode the first few waves easily. In a careless second the helmsman lowered the blade of the rear sweep too far into the rapids. The pull of the water was so strong and so sudden that the pilot, who had a fast hold on the sweep, was pulled out of the boat. That was not all. The sweep rebounded, knocking the passenger on the rear seat into the river too. Neither was drowned. But experiences like that make every Middle Fork guide cautious and careful.

The problem of each rapids is different at the various stages of Summer. In July, the best month to run the river, many ledges and rocks are covered that in August are exposed or close to the surface. A change of a few inches in water level creates new navigation hazards. That is why careful guides usually tie up at the head of major rapids and walk down the shore to study the depth of the slick, the size of the rollback, and the position of submerged rocks.

Greater risks come with high water. When the runoff of snow is at its peak, the Middle Fork rises seven feet or more. Then many ledges and sharp corners that present problems in July are rendered harmless. High water is dangerous. The torrent that pours through some of the funnels in the river at high water throws up rollbacks that no boat suitable for the Middle Fork can survive. These rollbacks flip a boat or swamp it. The history of the Middle Fork during the period of the runoffs is one of tragedy to boatmen. Prudent men do not run the Middle Fork when it is in flood.

Even in the low-water months of July and August there is one piece of white water that cannot be run. It is Sulphur Creek Rapids, sometimes known as Dagger Falls. It drops about twenty-five feet in fifty yards. In that drop it passes over two ledges. For small boats the risk of the sheer drop is forbidding. For larger boats the risk is not so much the drop as the ledges.

"I could clear the first ledge with my sweeps," Ralph says. "But one has to keep his sweeps in the white water to steer. If they ever hit that second ledge, I'd be finished."

Ralph lets his boat down Sulphur Creek Rapids on a 200-foot rope. Those who use smaller rubber boats or flat-bottomed wooden boats portage Sulphur Creek Rapids. Those who use the smaller boats do not attempt to run even Grouse Creek Rapids, but let their boats down on ropes instead. But Ralph runs them all except Sulphur Creek Rapids.

Each rapids has a foaming pool with different hydraulics. A few inches to the right or to the left makes the difference between success and tragedy. There is a thrill in doing it just right —and a satisfaction too.

Grouse Creek Rapids, which I described, was for me too breathless to enjoy. But as the days passed and I studied the river, I came to understand the engineering problems presented by each piece of white water. It was then a joy to see Ralph, a riverman in the best tradition, perform. He seemed to know exactly where the main thrust of the current was and where the boat need start its downward course in order to avoid the dangerous obstacles. I often watched him catch the main current inches from its center, and so avoid by a hair a dangerous ledge a dozen feet below. Often when we rode a rollback to the peak, it seemed that the boat would turn sideways. It was a thrill in that split second to feel Ralph catch a piece of spray with his rear sweep and straighten us out.

By the time we reached Granite Falls (sometimes called Dirty Drawers) my confidence in Ralph was unbounded. It was good that it was, for Granite Falls to me was the worst of them. Here the river drops eight feet. One enters the rapids over a wide ledge. The channel quickly narrows to a funnel that leads to a large rock on the right. There the water is deflected to the left for a few yards, where it pours onto another huge rock. The danger is in piling up on that second rock.

We dropped off the ledge with a sudden sucking sound and headed for the first rock. An easy touch of the sweeps fore and aft made us miss that rock by inches. Now we were in the main current, headed for the second rock. A touch of the rear sweep turned the nose to the right. The pitch of the stream raised the left side of the boat so that it tipped at a 45-degree angle. In that fashion we rode the roaring wall of water that poured off the right-hand side of the second rock. Not more than three or four seconds had passed since we entered the falls. But in that brief time Ralph had applied the precise pressure on the sweeps to avoid the two rocks and bring us into the clear.

In Porcupine Rapids we had climbed the main rollback and started down when Ralph was nearly thrown from the boat. "Got too big a bite of the white water with my rear sweep," he told me later. Both sweeps were knocked from his hands and Ralph went sprawling in the boat. He was up in a second and back on the deck. Yet in that second the boat had turned completely around in a trough and seemed doomed by an oncoming rollback.

Ralph Smothers was born to the river. His father, A. N. Smothers, has long been a riverman in Idaho. For years he ran the main Salmon River from Salmon City to Riggins. This river was the one that turned back Lewis and Clark, requiring them to take a tortuous overland route to the Snake River and the Columbia. It was on the main Salmon that Ralph, then ten years old, had his first experience with sweeps. He and his younger brother (killed in an airplane crash) were with their father on one of his runs down the main Salmon. The father fell and broke his ankle. They still had twenty miles of treacherous white water to run. Ten-year-old Ralph took the sweeps and under the guidance of his father, who sat at his feet, brought the boat through safely.

Ralph's first trip on the Middle Fork was also with his father. It was in the late thirties, when people in Idaho were still feeling the effects of the depression. There is some gold in the mountains of the Middle Fork—enough to keep a man in bread and beans. Ralph's father and another man went to look for it and took Ralph along. They searched much of the country to the west of the Middle Fork. They combed Big Creek, famous in history for skirmishes between the United States Army and the Sheepeater Indians, a branch of the Shoshones. Discouraged, they followed Big Creek to its junction with the Middle Fork, where they built a raft to run the thirty miles of the Middle Fork to the Salmon River. All the food they had left was coffee and rice. All went well until they hit Porcupine Rapids. There the raft was caught in a maelstrom of white water and broken in two. The passengers were thrown clear and managed to get to shore. They salvaged the pieces of the raft and the rice. Only the coffee was lost. In a few hours they had the raft repaired, and reached the main river in safety.

Ralph can make corn bread over a campfire that is as tasty as any in New Orleans. Though good-humored, he is a taciturn chap who seldom talks about himself. His wife, Rae, fills in the details. She seldom goes with Ralph on his trips, as she must stay with the children. When she goes she always gets wet. "You know," she said with a pleasant drawl, "I really think Ralph knows how to make a wave splash anyone in the boat."

Mercedes, remembering the times the waves had broken over us, looked at Ralph quizzically. Ralph grinned and said, "It would be no fun running the Middle Fork if you didn't get a little wet."

Changing the subject, he said, "You always got to figure that the boat will turn over."

"Did you figure that on our trip?" I asked.

"Sure I did," he answered. "Didn't you see my sleeping bag and air mattress wrapped up in that oilskin? I always keep a little air in my mattress, so the bed will float if we capsize."

One can reach the Middle Fork without too much trouble. There is a dirt road out of Stanley, Idaho, leading to Bear Valley Creek. Boats can be hauled to that point. Or one can shorten the trip by flying over 9000-foot ridges and landing on one of the meadows in the upper stretches of the river, taking his rubber boat in the plane. That is what we did. It took three trips from Salmon City to Indian Creek in a Cessna plane, piloted by Mike Loening, to bring us and all our supplies to the Middle Fork. In four hours the job was finished. We could have packed in with horses. But that would have taken days. And time is precious on the Middle Fork in July, when the water is neither too low nor too high.

Once one reaches the Middle Fork he is in solitude that is profound. The canyon walls, studded with granite cliffs, rise a mile or more. Sometimes they rise sheer a thousand feet. The upper reaches are carved into great, spacious bowls. This region has an interesting geological history. Some 40 million years ago it had been reduced by erosion to gentle contours. Then came the uplift, marked first by the intrusion of granite and later by basalt. During the glacial period the valleys had not yet been cut deep and narrow like a V. The grinding of the ice was felt only at what now are the higher altitudes—mostly above 6500 feet. These glaciers gouged out deep amphitheatrical recesses that now stand out like big bowls above the narrow stream bed.

After the ice receded, the narrow stream beds were cut by erosion. The land above the river, shaped into great basins and capped by granite crags, has only a few slopes that are heavily wooded. This is mostly open counry with scatterings of trees and much sagebrush.

There are blue grouse and bobwhites on the slopes and, closer to the river, some ruffed grouse. High up on the ridges and in the bowls grow the white pine and, somewhat lower, the Engelmann's spruce. Down along the waterway are mostly the tenacious black pine, the dignified yellow pine, and the stately Douglas fir. Clumps of aspen often occupy a ravine. Here, too, is the brilliant fireweed. An occasional cottonwood grows near the water's edge, along with stands of willow. Streaks of mountain alder follow streams down the canyon slopes. Huckleberries grow here; so does the elderberry, snowberry, and the wild rose. There are scatterings of hawthorn along the Middle Fork, and here and there a hackberry, a chokeberry, and a cascara shrub. One can find Oregon grape and perhaps a Johnny-jump-up. Up and down the canyon are stands of mountain mahogany that elk and deer like for browse. And in the lower reaches of the river the juniper known as Rocky Mountain Red Cedar grows.

Trails touch the river at some points. But not many people travel them these days. There are two dude ranches along the Middle Fork—McCall's and the Flying B Ranch. Yet they are not greatly used. An occasional prospector's cabin still stands. But none is occupied; and the claims once worked have mostly been acquired by the Forest Service.

The result is a 130-mile stretch of white water in a canyon of a remote wilderness. The water is clear, pure, and cold. There are white sand bars without number, where one can make camp under a yellow pine or Douglas fir. In the lower reaches there

are rattlesnakes on the ledges above the river. But the sand bars are clear of insects and snakes. These sand bars are filled with enough driftwood to satisfy generations of campers. And I remember some where mountain mahogany, once pressed down by heavy snow, grows almost parallel with the ground and furnishes a convenient roof for sleeping bags. These sand bars have no sign of civilization on them—not even the tin cans and cardboard boxes which usually mark the impact of man on a wilderness. But their fringes are decorated with an occasional blue gentian or some lupine, or perhaps a larkspur. And miner's lettuce and a monkey flower may be found in a shaded, moist place.

Up and down the Middle Fork there are mineral hot springs where deer and sheep come for salting. Here the Sheepeater Indians used to bathe. And today an ingenious traveler can find himself a hot shower bath.

The Middle Fork is one of the finest fishing streams in America. It has cutthroat trout that run up to three pounds and rainbow that run to two pounds. Occasionally a Dolly Varden is caught, and they have been known to run to five pounds. Steelhead and salmon also run the river, coming hundreds of miles from the Pacific to this remote Idaho stream to perform the ritual of spawning.

The prize of the summer fisherman is cutthroat or rainbow trout, both native to the stream. They are so abundant, a party could not possibly eat what its members catch. Our practice was to throw back everything we caught before four o'clock, even the one- or two-pounders. The fishing is so good that there is a drive on by conservationists to ban salmon eggs, spinners, and all bait from the river. The plan is to make the Middle Fork exclusively a fly-fishing stream. Even the fly brings more to the net than one can eat. We used the fly exclusively, concentrating on the bee and caddis patterns. I often fished the flies dry, quartering the river upstream and taking a long float. But I also caught many fish on the reprieve when the fly was wet. The truth is that these Middle Fork trout will strike almost anything that moves or floats. Their pools are rarely disturbed by man. They have not yet developed the wariness of trout that are hunted all Summer long.

There are interesting caves along the Middle Fork. We saw one that was sixty feet long and twenty feet wide. Another lay under an overhang of a granite cliff. Both had petroglyphs on the rock walls. They were made years ago by the Sheepeaters. Those Indians were never more than 200 strong. They were renegades who escaped to the safety of the Middle Fork and lived in its caves, eating mountain sheep and elk that they killed with bows and arrows and skinned with obsidian knives.

No Sheepeaters are left today. They were defeated by the United States Army in 1879 in one of the most difficult military campaigns we have conducted, and were shipped off to an Indian Reservation. Only the writings on the walls of the caves give any clue that man once lived here.

A few years ago Ralph Smothers spent three weeks in the Middle Fork with a man who was dying of cancer. A friend brought the sick man there. The three of them floated the Middle Fork leisurely, so that the dying man could know the full glory of this world before he passed on. There is, indeed, no finer sanctuary in America. The Middle Fork is substantially the wilderness it was a hundred years ago. Its forests have not been cut. The canyons are so remote and so treacherous there has been precious little grazing by cattle and sheep. The few planes that use its meadows have not altered its character. It abounds in game—deer, elk, bear, bobcat, cougar, coyote, mountain sheep, and mountain goat. There are even moose here; and there are also marten, muskrat, mink, and weasel. There are some fresh tracks on every sand bar.

Most of the game is high among the breaks in Summer, coming down late in the Fall. During the ten days we spent in the majestic canyon we saw none except mountain sheep. These sheep are very nervous to any movement above them. An appearance of man on heights that overlook them creates a panic. As long as man stays below them he can approach quite close. One afternoon we spotted ewes and rams on a bench overlooking the river. There were a couple dozen of them, mostly bedded down, only a few grazing. Ralph steered the raft so that we would pass below them. We skimmed the side of the cliff showing stands of a purple penstemon. The sheep were not more than fifteen feet above us. Yet not a one moved.

Back in Salmon City I talked with W. H. Shaw, Supervisor of the Salmon National Forest, about the Middle Fork. His eyes lighted up as he talked of the plans to make this a real wilderness area.

"It's so rugged that trails are not much use. We put all our fire fighters in by parachute these days," he said.

"How do you get them out?" I asked.

"We instruct them to return to the river, where a boat will pick them up," he answered.

The one who will pick them up will be Ralph Smothers, or one of a half-dozen other men who know its white water.

Back in Washington, D.C., I learned that there are engineering plans on file to put as many as nineteen separate dams along the Middle Fork in order to harness it for hydroelectric power.

Those of us who have traveled the Middle Fork think this would be the greatest indignity ever inflicted on a sanctuary. The Middle Fork—one of our finest wilderness areas—must be preserved in perpetuity.

Man and his great dams have frequently done more harm than good. Margaret Hindes put the idea in beautiful verse:

> Gone, desecrated for a dam—
> Pines, stream, and trails
> Burned and bared
> Down to dust.
> Now water fills the hollow,
> Water for power,
> But the bowl of wilderness
> Is broken, forever.

I discussed this matter with Olaus J. Murie. "We pay farmers *not* to produce certain crops," I said. "Why not pay the Army Engineers *not* to build dams?"

Olaus laughed and said, "Good idea." And he went on to add that soon all dams for hydroelectric power will be obsolete.

We are, indeed, on the edge of new breakthroughs that will open up sources of power that will make it unnecessary, and indeed foolhardy, to build more dams across our rivers *to produce power*. Hydrogen fusion, with an energy potential that is astronomical, has not yet been mastered. But it certainly will be. Solar energy, though not yet available by commercial standards, is in the offing. Nuclear fission already exists and promises enormous energy supplies. Science may yet save the sanctuary of the Middle Fork from destruction.

CHAPTER IV

HART MOUNTAIN

Hart Mountain—thirty miles long—rises like a gargantuan loaf from the dry prairies of southeastern Oregon. Its main ridges are over 7000 feet high; Warner Peak, its southernmost point, reaches nearly 8100 feet. This is a mountain of lava rock whose cliffs show streaks of yellow and red. The west and the north sides are almost sheer walls that drop precipitously 3000 feet to Warner Valley that is as smooth as a table top. The valley is dotted with marshy lakes, which trappers of the Hudson's Bay

Company called *lacs des plants*. They are, indeed, rich in tules, sedges, and pond weeds. The rugged northern wall has been fenced off as a vast pasture for bighorn sheep, which once occupied this range and recently have been reintroduced. The east and south sides have easier slopes. The east slope rises gently; the south is broken by moderately level benches. The whole of Hart Mountain and much of the valley land to the south and east make up the Hart Mountain Antelope Refuge, established in 1936.

The pronghorned antelope is truly American in ancestry, having lived here for some millions of years. It is small, as horned ruminants go, the does averaging a little over 90 pounds and the bucks 114 pounds. The antelope is faster than any of its other relatives. I once clocked a Hart Mountain antelope at 60 miles an hour. This American antelope—cinnamon-brown and white—is different from other horned ruminants in other respects also. It is the only one that has hollow horns; and it sheds the outer shell once a year. Its hair, which is hollow, is so controlled by muscles that it can be made to lie flat or to stand up. This gives the animal the power to retain warmth in the Winter or to arrange its pelage in a cooling pattern for the hot days of Summer. Thus it can remain comfortable whether the temperature is 20°F. below zero or 120°F. above. Moreover, the eyes of the antelope have an extraordinarily wide angle of vision, being able to see behind them as well as in front and to catch the slightest movement on a distant horizon. Its saucy white rump flashing over the prairie is probably as distinctively American as anything our wilderness offers.

Hart Mountain, with pronghorned antelopes at its base, is, therefore, a choice sanctuary.

My first climb of Hart Mountain is in memory like a haunting melody. This is an exotic ridge, different from any I have known. Guano Plateau stretches to the south and east as far as the eye can see. The rainfall is not more than ten inches annually. Here is a vast expanse of dry, windblown land that to the untrained eye paints a picture of desolation. One can look to the horizon and see no tree except an occasional western juniper. Far to the southeast Steens Mountains lie against the skyline—a great hulk of land with a bluish tinge. On the plateau there are light green spots that from a distance look like pastures. They are called lakes— Spanish Lake, Desert Lake, Flook Lake—because water gathers there in the Spring. But by June they are dry, and the antelope feed there during the summer months. A type of salt grass, known as alkali sacaton, grows in these lake beds. The antelope eat some of it. But when they forgather at these lakes they usually come to eat the plants and blossoms of the yellow flowered prim- rose and other wild flowers that flourish there.

The Idaho fescue grows on these plains. There is also the Sandberg (or little) bluegrass and the famous blue-bunch wheat- grass for which the dry slopes of the Pacific Northwest are famous. These are excellent forage for the antelope. There is also the cheat grass that invades the ranges of the West on the heels of overgrazing. The antelope eat it when it starts up in the Fall after the rains.

The antelope consume the flowers and leaves of the lupine and desert clovers, and even the blossoms of the death camass. And for winter forage they rely mainly on rabbit brush, bitter brush, and sagebrush. These latter are, indeed, an important item in the antelope's diet the year around. Studies by Olaus J. Murie show that sagebrush and other browse plants are vital to the prong- horned antelope as well as to the sage grouse. So it is alarming to those who want these species perpetuated to hear of proposals for the removal of sagebrush from Hart Mountain.

A large shoulder of the mountain, thick with sagebrush, recently caught fire by accident, and hundreds of acres were burned. Bunch grass took over on the heels of the fire, and this shoulder now boasts a thick stand of it. Some want to burn or spray other sagebrush areas to bring on richer stands of grass. This is good news to cattlemen, who enjoy grazing rights in this refuge. The political pressures are toward improving the ranges of Hart Mountain for cattle grazing as, under federal law, Lake County, where the refuge is located, gets 25 per cent of all grazing fees earned by the refuge; and that amount goes into the local school and road fund. Though it amounts to only a few thousand dollars a year, the allies against sagebrush are powerful. This promises no good for either the antelope or the sage grouse. For as grass invades, the margin of subsistence for wildlife dependent on sagebrush narrows. If we are to give antelope the preference they deserve, sagebrush and the other browse on which they are dependent must be allowed to flourish.

The plains at the base of Hart Mountain are in the Upper Sonoran life zone. Here will be found, along with the sage grouse, hawks, horned owls, ash-throated flycatchers, gray flycatchers, bushtits, and Oregon lark sparrows. And among the mammals there are, in addition to the pronghorned antelopes, rabbits, chipmunks, ground squirrels, mice, coyotes, and skunks.

As one climbs Hart Mountain he enters three other life zones. The Transition zone is characterized by the ponderosa pine. It harbors a great variety of birds—Oregon poorwill, nighthawks, flickers, woodpeckers, western wood pewee, warblers, robins, western chipping sparrow, Warner Mountain fox sparrow, and valley quail.

The Canadian zone starts around 6500 feet, and during the wet seasons carries snow well into the Summer. This is the home of the cony, Arizona weasel, golden-mantled ground squirrel, and western white-tailed jack rabbit. Here are forests of quaking aspen and thickets of willow, mountain mahogany, mountain alder, and wild gooseberries. The western goshawk, red-naped sapsucker, mountain bluebird, Oregon white-crowned sparrows, and meadowlarks make this their habitat.

At about 7500 feet the Hudsonian zone commences. There the aspen and mountain mahogany have thinned out, leaving most of the top open and exposed. Some of the mammals of the Canadian zone are found here and many of the birds, particularly the sparrows and bluebirds.

It was mid-July when I first climbed Hart Mountain. Most of the bloom had left the plateau. Only yellow desert snowballs and wild onions were flowering there. Higher up I came across some startling wild-flower effects. In open places on the lower shoulder of the mountain I found fields of the delicate rose-colored Clarkia, the flower that Lewis and Clark first discovered on the Clearwater in Idaho and which bears the name of Captain William Clark. David Douglas rediscovered this Clarkia on the Columbia and sent it to England.

I had not gone far before I came across a hillside of the green-banded mariposa lily—with three lavender and lilac petals whose yellow base is dotted with dark purple and violet spots. Scattered lavishly among these lilies were the waxen blooms of the delicate bitterroot. The soft, bright colors of the flowers and their delicacy were in vivid contrast to the heavy dullness and coarseness of the sage.

At about 6500 feet I found hundreds of acres of lupine in

bloom—mostly blue but some white and some mixed. It stood at times almost knee-high, dominating the bunch grass with which it grew. As I climbed higher I came across patches of soft pink alpine phlox, clinging tenaciously to sandy outcroppings as if it had pledged its life to prevent even the coarse topsoil from blowing away.

This had been a late summer, and the grasses—fescue, squirreltail, and native bunch—were thick and lush. Near the top I sat down among them. There was lupine at my feet, and at my back was a small stand of mountain mahogany. The mahogany, which stood about eight feet high, had a bushlike appearance, and its top had been browsed upon so much by deer and antelope that it looked as if it had been carefully clipped with shears by some meticulous gardener.

Below me lay the Guano Plateau, stretching almost a hundred miles to the Steens Mountains on the far horizon. The dry lakes of the plateau gave a light greenish touch to the somber gray and dust of the sage. Long fingers of greasewood were thrust out into the sage, marking the places where the soil is alkaline. Darker green dots were scattered in a patternless scheme across the plateau. These marked the western juniper, the tree that is good for fuel and fence posts in this vast and empty domain.

The view from the top of Hart Mountain creates a feeling of greater depth and expanse than even the Great Plains. Valleys are as flat as a table top for seventy-five miles. The land is bleak and gray. Yet a shimmer of blue against the skyline says that there is water to be had. A streak of green along a distant hillside tells of springs and creeks. Patches of light green across the plateaus show where the rich native hay grows. And one has only to watch the plateau through glasses or walk through its sagebrush to learn that it virtually teems with life. This is land to possess and embrace. It is land to command as far as the eye can see. Here is the ultimate for the possessive instinct.

Across a ravine a buck antelope was standing in the open, alternately burying his nose in sagebrush and scanning the slopes for signs of danger. A mule deer crossed the field below me and then, sensing danger, ran for a cover of mahogany.

The late Stanley Jewett counted 120 species of birds on Hart Mountain, and the list is not yet complete. Not far below the point where I was resting I had seen a black-chinned humming-bird feeding its young in a nest on the side of an aspen. Now a turkey buzzard was circling below me, looking for carrion. Farther down, a grebe was flying east to some nesting grounds. A few ducks streaked by as if they were frantically trying to find their flock before day's end. I looked up, and there in the sky—perhaps a mile above me—were white objects flying in wide circles. These were white pelicans that nest in the Malheur National Wild Life Refuge some miles to the east. Now they were wheeling in great circles ten thousand feet or more above Guano Plateau. They were promenading in the sky like a fleet of bombers on display.

I also climbed Hart Mountain in the dry cycle when Guano Plateau was parched and even the grass on the slopes was suffering. I camped under ponderosa pine by clear and cold Guano creek where the Order of the Antelope has its annual outing. This group, formed to honor and perpetuate the refuge, had forgathered; and Samuel M. Smith, business executive from California who also loves Hart Mountain, and I sat in the shade listening to officials of the refuge give an accounting of this dry cycle. The dry season had not noticeably affected the deer population. They have, indeed, become so abundant that the refuge is open to hunters. Hunting deer by bow and arrow is permitted; and the archers have a success ratio of less than eight per cent. The drought, however, had a very serious effect on the pronghorns. The antelope herd had been down to 100 before the refuge was established in 1936. When I first visited the area, the herd had increased to 2000. The dry cycle of the late fifties had reduced them to 700. The dry cycle was proving that Hart Mountain as a refuge was necessary if antelope were to survive.

This time I climbed the mountain via Stockade Creek, one of the few streams that run off these ridges. At the point where Stockade Creek pours onto the plateau the antelope were gathering for food and water. When feed and water are plentiful they tend to scatter. Now they were bunching in herds of 100 and more—one evidence of the dry cycle. This creek, which rises at about 7000 feet from a spring in the mountain's side, has clear, cold water. Aspen line its banks nearly to the source. I was serenaded most of the way by meadowlarks. I found the dainty water spring beauty in wet spots along the creek bed. Large yellow monkey flowers nodded in the light, hot breeze that touched the ravine. The royal blue penstemon flourished here. The tiny, petty cinquefoil bowed graciously.

The blue American speedwell, so petite as to seem unreal, grew here. Along with it was the tansyleaf evening primrose—a bright yellow flower almost concealed by its tall serrated leaves. By its side was the gay spike checkermallow with an inflorescence of purple flowers.

As I left the creek bed and climbed the gentle slopes to Warner Peak, I found new glories of this mountain. First was the Wyoming paintbrush, flower of the State of Wyoming—orange-red against the dull sage. Yellow eriogonum were splashed lavishly across the mountain. Even though this was a drought year, the lovely mariposa lily—lavender with purple dots on its sepals—was flourishing in the shade of the sage. Another delicate creation was the longstalk starwort, whose single tiny white flower seemed almost out of keeping with the harshness of the sage. Perhaps loveliest of all were the scatterings of the western blue flax, whose bright blue flowers get protection from the shade of the sage. This is the flower that served the Indians well by providing them with cordage. It bears the name of Lewis of the Lewis and Clark Expedition.

Farther up Stockade Creek I found other evidences of the dry cycle. The golden-mantled ground squirrel was beginning to hibernate, though July was not ended. And the sage grouse had moved far up the mountain. As I worked my way along the ravine they went out from under my feet in large numbers. One covey of forty-two broke the stillness of the mountain with the roar of a bomber plane. Young hens weighing a couple of pounds escaped gracefully. Old toms weighing over five pounds worked hard to get elevation.

There were antelope fawn in the aspen groves, born in June. When the rabbits and rodents are in low supply, the predators turn to these fawn. The coyote and the golden eagle are the chief enemies. They actually follow an antelope doe until she discloses where the fawn is located or until the fawn makes a false move. But predator control is necessary only two years out of ten. Most of the time, nature supplies the necessary balance. Wildlife will continue to have its periods of decline and its periods of prosperity. As yet we do not know all the factors that play a role in these cycles. Food, of course, is important. And if we have sense enough to heed Dr. Murie's warning and leave the sagebrush unmolested, we will have done much to insure against the decline and extinction of the antelope.

I was thinking of these things as I last stood on the top of Hart Mountain, watching the lengthening shadows streak across the plateau far below me. It struck me that man sometimes seems to try to crowd everything but himself out of the universe. Yet he cannot live a full life from the products of his own creation. He needs a measure of the wilderness, so that he may relax in the environment that God made for him. He needs life around him in order to experience the true measure of living. Then only can he get a sense of the full glory of the universe. There is a place in man's life for the antelope, just as there is for the whir of sage grouse and the song of the thrush. There would be a great emptiness in the land if there were no pelicans wheeling in great circles over Hart Mountain, no antelope fawn in its aspen groves, no red-shafted flickers in its willow. I say the same for the coyote and golden eagle. We often downgrade them as predators. Yet they, too, play an important role in the cosmic scheme.

I always feel sad leaving Hart Mountain. Yet after I travel a few hours and turn to see its great bulk against a southern sky my heart rejoices. This refuge will leave our grandsons and grand-daughters an inheritance of the wilderness that no dollars could recreate. Here they will find life teeming throughout all the life zones that lead from the desert to alpine meadows.

Those who visit Hart Mountain next century will know that we were faithful life tenants, that we did not entirely despoil the earth which we left them. We will make the tradition of con-servation as much a part of their inheritance as the land itself.

CHAPTER V

MOUNT ADAMS

THIS Fall the cones of the pine and fir produced a scant crop of seeds; and state and federal men were scouring the Mount Adams area looking for healthy cones to fill their gunnysacks. Seeds were needed for the nurseries of the Northwest, and this year good ones were hard to find.

Some think that the winter temperatures have something to do with the cycles of good and poor seeds. Their theory is that when the Winters are severe, with long periods below freezing, the insects that infest these cones do not survive. When the Winter is mild, like last Winter, the insects get a new lease on life and are thriving by Spring. Others think that, so far as cone and seed insects are concerned, the effect of temperature on them is slight. These insects have their cycles. Their Golden Age comes and goes; they have their ups and downs, their periods of prosperity and depression. The factors affecting their abundance are many. This school doubts that temperature plays a significant role.

I sat one night on the lawn of our summer place at the foot of Mount Adams, listening to some forester friends discuss these problems of ecology. The relation of living things to each other, the effect one has on another are an endless interplay. Nature in the ecologic sense seems bent on maintaining a balance which will disenable any one of its creations from gaining dominance over the rest. When hawks have plentiful supplies of rodents and outbreed their inferiors, the ecologic results of starvation start operating until a balance between hawks and rodents is again established. The same is true of coyotes and rabbits, cougar and deer, lynx and fox. These things I knew as a boy. Later in life I came to know something of the balance between aspen and birch on one hand and beaver on the other, between willow and other browse and deer and elk. In Oregon I had come to know how overpopulation of elk and deer on certain ranges was death to mountain mahogany—and to the elk and deer too.

Now I was learning that, in the cosmic scheme of the woods, insects have the same place as other animals.

There is a nice ecological balance between insects and the cones and seeds of trees. The ponderosa pine is host to many insects. There are white hairy grubs, small pink maggots, rose-colored caterpillars, and yellow-white larvae that destroy the

cones and seeds of the tree. But the worst of all are small brown scolytid beetles and pith moths.

The larvae of the pith moths bore through the cone to the seeds and then pass from seed to seed, feeding on the kernels. They have been the greatest destroyer of ponderosa seed in the Northwest. This last year, that was so unfavorable to the cones and seed of this pine, these pith moths destroyed more than 50 per cent of all the pine seed destroyed in the Glenwood area.

The scolytid beetle enters the cone by piercing the scales close to the base of the cone. Then it bores completely around the axis of the cone, cutting off its nourishment and insuring the deadening of the cone. That process is necessary for its purpose, since it needs a dead cone for an egg gallery and the development of its larvae.

The pith moths develop parasites that help contain them. But neither the beetle nor the moth has known predators.

Quite different insects favor cones and seeds of the Douglas fir. One of the worst is a chalcid, or wasp, that lays its eggs in a young seed—a not too easy task, since the Douglas fir cone is pendent, which places the female in a difficult position. There are two moths that raise havoc with the cones and seeds of the Douglas fir. Their larvae dig elaborate food channels in the cone, eating the seeds they encounter and causing the cones to wither, with the result that the seed crop does not mature. Numerous parasites help control these moths, but there are no known predators for either them or for the chalcids. When warm Winters come, these wasps and moths more than hold their own, upsetting the cone and seed balance in the Douglas fir. That at least is the theory of some foresters.

No destructive species continues indefinitely in epidemic numbers. The parasites and predators bring insects under control. The food supply of the insects also falls off. They would be exterminated by this process except for one device nature has designed. These insects for the most part do not all emerge from winter hibernation. Some hold over a year, some two years. Biologists recognize that this diapause is nature's key to the survival of these lowly and—to man—despicable species.

The bark beetle that infests the Engelmann's spruce is more clearly controlled by low temperatures. Studies show -30°F. is necessary to kill all the beetles and all the larvae. In 1939 high winds blew down many big spruce trees in Colorado. These trees, covered with snow, were warm homes for these insects. Beetles under the snow were also protected from predators, particularly the downy, the hairy, and the arctic three-toed woodpeckers. This protection gave the bark beetles such a head start that before their cycle was closed they had killed five billion cubic feet of timber.

From 1939 to 1945 the bark beetles ravaged these spruce forests in the Routt National Forest and the White River National Forest. Once the beetles finished a forest and then migrated, crossing thirty-five miles of open sagebrush country to invade a new stand of spruce. Forest Service spraying helped turn the tide. Parasites and predators that feed off the larvae of the bark beetle also helped. Nematodes that enter the digestive tract of the beetle and reduce the fertility of the female played a hand. So did an extremely cold winter. But while the bark beetles were enjoying their Golden Age, the woodpeckers were increasing. The increased food supply boosted the woodpecker population. They too played a part in bringing the Golden Age of the bark beetle to a close and restoring the ecological balance in favor of the Engelmann's spruce. During this epidemic period, spruce beetle larvae and adults constituted as high as 91 per cent of the woodpeckers' winter food and 65 per cent of their summer food.

What worries the foresters in the Mount Adams country most is the western pine beetle. This seems to be the No. 1 enemy of the ponderosa pine. It breeds in overmature trees, unhealthy trees, windfalls, or trees that have been weakened by drought or fires. Under epidemic conditions it attacks vigorous trees of all ages. This beetle is a tiny one about ⅛ to ⅕ inch long. It is monogamous and builds egg galleries under the bark. There are about two generations of these beetles annually in the Mount Adams country. They cause losses as high as 50 per cent of the ponderosa pine over a five-year period. They have natural enemies—two other beetles and our woodpecker friends. Prolonged low winter temperatures from 20°F. below zero on down also help reduce this pine beetle. The last few warm Winters in the Mount Adams country promise an epidemic of the pine-bark beetle this next Spring. The foresters are already talking about sanitation and salvage logging, by which the high-risk trees are removed from the forest and utilized for lumber, thus depriving the pine-bark beetles of susceptible host materials.

Man has done many things in the realm of ecologic control and adaptation, the vaccine against poliomyelitis being most conspicuous. Modern science has gone far toward establishing the basis for coexistence between man and various bacteria and viruses, casting the balance in favor of the inoculated individual. In the Far West various insecticide sprays have been used on some trees, notably the Douglas fir and Engelmann's spruce. This ecological manipulation may sometimes work. Yet it has decided limitations; each victory for man sets forces of reaction into play. The "germ" that the vaccine destroyed develops an immunity, and so a new vaccine must be found. The process appears to be an endless one. For ecologic nature apparently plays no favorites; it strives to keep all of its creatures in some kind of balance. It is not always successful, for new species do emerge and old ones disappear. But each has a competitive place in the cosmic scheme. There has been some niche reserved for the scolytid beetle; and no matter the barriers erected he, like the vibrio of cholera or the bacillus of tuberculosis, will probably survive.

The sun had left the snow fields of Mount Adams and Jupiter was out before we ended our discussion. The symbiosis—or intimate association—of insects and the pine placed in new dimension the silent struggle for existence which goes on in every forest.

This Adams country is an old familiar friend. I hiked most of it as a boy, carrying a pack. I have fished its high lakes, slept on its shoulders, eaten its lush blueberries, stalked its deer, sampled its grouse, and listened to the music of its conifers.

It was on and around Mount Adams that I had, as a boy, the experience that Marguerite J. Adams has put in poetry:

> Why should there be this urge for farther heights,
> distant horizons that he cannot know?
> The trail is steep, the branches that he fights
> retards his way; birches and hemlocks grow
> beside his shoulders; here a fallen log
> holds him a moment, tasting mountain fog.
>
> Wind-blown his hair, as at a final turn
> he steps upon the summit he has sought;
> factual vision that will ever burn
> above the lower plain where he was caught
> and made escape, and by such climbing grew
> beyond the world of childhood that he knew.

I climb it from the south side and learn that it, too, is fragile and fleeting. This great basalt uplift is crumbling and the rate must be fast, geologically speaking, for it is noticeable in my life span. Whole slopes on Mount Adams are made up of pyro-clastics—ashes, cinders, pumice, and bombs produced by an extinct volcano. Some of these rocks are filled with air holes, and so light they will float for awhile in water. All of them make treacherous underfooting. They travel like shale, new pieces being constantly added to the descending rocks through the operation of frost, snow, and ice.

When I was a boy I could see Mount Adams from our front porch in Yakima. Nowadays I can see it from my home in Glen-wood. It is snow-capped the year around and shows various moods depending on the weather. On the clear days of Summer it is resplendent in the bright rays of morning. Before a storm moves in from the west, the mountain seems to tower in dark rage. The fires that come when the humidity drops and the forests dry out sometimes cast a pall of smoke over the land. Then Mount Adams has softer lines and is distant and indistinct, a mountain of mystery. If the sun sets clear, there is a moment before the mountain is swallowed up by darkness when it is brightly luminous, incandescent, a startling ball of cold light. When the full moon rises, the distant snow fields dimly reflect a golden glow. Then the mountain seems so far, so remote, as to belong to another world.

My home is at 2000 feet elevation. Mount Adams is 12,307 feet. Though it towers nearly two miles above me, I may not see it for hours on end as I travel this mountain area, for the trail is usually beneath a ridge. Yet when I travel there I almost feel the presence of the mountain. I am filled with the expectancy of seeing it from every height of land, at every opening of a canyon. And the sight of its black basalt cliffs crowned with white snow, both set against a blue sky, is enough to make a man stop in wonderment. Sometimes as I travel around Mount Adams counterclockwise from the south I will be in the canyon of the Klickitat River for twenty miles or more. As the dirt road crosses a shoulder of a ridge, I may get a fleeting glimpse of Mount Adams—perhaps only a view of its rounded dome. But even that is enough to lift the heart.

The view of Adams best known is from the south, for the main arteries of travel are there. It was from that direction that Lewis and Clark saw it, calling it a "high humped" mountain. It does have a setback below the summit which to a climber creates the impression of a false top. The view I like most is the less familiar one from the north. From that angle Adams is black rock draped with glaciers, capped with snow, and set against a deep blue sky.

I like to take the dirt road out of Glenwood and travel the canyon of the Klickitat about twenty miles to Soda Springs Creek that comes in from the west. The road is far above the Klickitat River, so far as to catch none of its roar. But its white waters can be seen now and then a thousand feet or more down steep slopes. Glenwood is spotted with ponderosa pine, the yellow-bellied beauty that the lumbermen like. But one headed up the Klickitat canyon soon leaves the yellow pine behind and reaches the firs.

I park the jeep under a huge Douglas fir on Soda Springs Creek and take the steep trail to Mount Adams Lake. While the trail travels about four miles northwest, it climbs one-half mile or more. Almost every step is up. There is open shade under the conifers that cover the slopes. This is the eastern side of the Cascades. The western slopes catch most of the moisture that drips from the clouds drifting in from the Pacific. Their undergrowth is thick. But the forests on the eastern slopes have an open effect. The trees, except for occasional thick stands of spindly lodgepole pine, are scattered. Pine grass grows in between. This grass, which is not very nutritious to grazing animals, is tall, broad leaved, and slick to walk on. Willow grows along Soda Springs Creek. And on the drier slopes the snowbrush, whose leaves have a resinous varnish, grows in extensive stands. The Indians once used the leaves for a tobacco. They are tough and have a glossy finish; and if rubbed together in water, they will produce a soapy lather. This bush, which is low-grade browse for deer and elk, fills the Klickitat Canyon with its fragrance in late June and July. It's a penetrating odor more subtle than any I know except the wild honeysuckle that flourishes in the Potomac River basin. This shrub, which the local people often call chaparral, is too thick for a horse. The deer love to bed down in it. Its roots place a protective shield over much of the eastern slopes of Mount Adams.

In late Spring and early Summer these eastern and northern slopes of the mountain are a riot of color. Most of the western wild flowers can be found there. Kinnikinnick covers much of the forest floor. July finds the ocean spray in bloom. The real Scotch bluebell is present with gaiety and nobility. The scarlet gilia nods in the shade. The wild rose and mountain teaberry are in bloom. The lovely twin flower stands graciously above the litter of the forest. Lupine and asters still decorate open slopes. A monkey flower or a spring beauty can be found in the wet shade. But the purplish pasque-flower, or western anemone, whose oval plumes look as delicate as gossamer is in seed. Every time I see this lovely creature, whether in flower or seed, I think of Aldo Leopold's dictum, "The chance to find a pasque-flower is a right as inalienable as free speech."

After one clears the ridge and just before he reaches Mount Adams Lake, he comes to a meadow where a spring offers clear, ice-cold water. We are now over 4500 feet high. Yet if one comes in August, the grass has begun to turn brown; and there's so much grazing by sheep that it's easy to stir up dust.

One comes to the lake quickly and without warning. It is like walking suddenly into the presence of something infinitely precious and beautiful. Several hundred acres of water are deep blue against the somber setting of conifers. Towering over it from the southwest is the mountain that Indian legend says was once a god named Klickitat. When the wind is down and the lake calm, the image of the mountain is in the lake. The reflection is so clear, the details so precise, that the image seems real. I have sat for hours in the shade of alpine fir at Mount Adams Lake watching the mountain in the lake. On the darkest, dreariest days of winter the picture comes back to me.

I have stepped into Mount Adams Lake, wearing my waders, and fished twenty-five feet or more from shore where the water is just under the arm pits. When the breeze is up and ripples cover the lake, this is the time for the fly fisherman. The prizes of this lake are worth waiting for. Rainbow trout as brilliant as the sunset and weighing four pounds have come to my net in these waters.

North of Mount Adams Lake about twenty miles or so lies Fish Lake, where eighteen- and twenty-four-inch fighting rainbow cruise. I have fished it with Elon Gilbert, who has walked these trails with me since boyhood, and with Sandy Balcom, musician, pantomimist, storyteller, and devotee of Isaac Walton. We caught a rainbow on almost every cast. At the south end is a thick stand of water lilies. The rainbow trout come out from under that cover to strike a fly with such viciousness that my heart stands still. This is a remote lake and a unique one, for it lies fifteen hundred feet or more deep in a narrow ravine, and for that drop the trail zigzags a mile or more. It's a hole whose sides are steep hills, thick and somber with conifers. Mount Adams is lost to sight. The sun sets early. And the view is so restricted that I feel confined, a rare experience for the mountains.

Two Lakes that lie five miles or so west of Fish Lake offer a different prospect. They lie under basalt cliffs, and the conifers are so thick there are no exciting views. But the trip into them, if one comes from the south, is as interesting a hike as I can wish for in any mountains. Wooded slopes make up the first part of the walk. Then come a series of meadows—four in number—which in recent geological time were probably lakes. They are still marshy; the grass is tall and lush, the penstemon bright blue. Even as late as August there are paintbrush and cinquefoil left. A yellow monkey flower is almost certain to be found. One who looks carefully will find the shooting star. Here and there are stands of the cotton grass. But more spectacular still are the views of Mount Adams from these marshy meadows. It is never seen full length; only its shoulders are in evidence. It seems, how-ever, to be only a stone's throw away from the low ridge on the meadow's far side. This towering black rock, powdered with white snow and set against a deep blue sky, is never so near, so intimate, as it is in these meadows. There is enough glory in one of these hikes to tide a man over the dark days.

As I return from Two Lakes, cross the meadows, and climb out of the valley, I come to the large basin which is part of the skirts of Mount Adams. This is the 6000-foot zone, where most of the timber has been left behind. Only alpine fir and some white pine are present. The impression is one of openness, not dense woods. That feeling is heightened by Mount Adams, which now

stands stark and massive, close at hand. The basin also gives a good
view to the north, where Mount Rainier (14,408 feet) stands in
stately splendor on a clear day. In between are the five peaks of
the Goat Rocks, reaching like fingers to the sky. And to the
west is a rounded dome—mostly clear of timber but marked by
a few charred stumps—known, by reason of its shape, as Potato
Hill.

I knew Potato Hill as a boy. It was then a good ten days' hike
from civilization. The hike was worth it because of the blueberries as well as the view. Here are the finest stands of blueberries in the Cascades. In the early days I would see Indian
squaws with horses carrying five-gallon kerosene cans loaded
with this delicious fruit and headed east for the Yakima Valley.
Then, as now, this was part of the Yakima Indian Reservation.
But today there are jeep roads clear to Potato Hill. When August
comes and the blueberries ripen, the Indians come by jeep to
camp and pick berries. The basin is a wide one—perhaps a mile
across—and spacious enough to accommodate many camps. There
is only one spring. But these are happy, carefree people who do
not mind walking a mile for a bucket of water.

The blueberry season has for them almost religious overtones.
They indulge it as they would a rite. Men and women come to
Potato Hill and camp for days and even weeks. One day this
last Summer I stood on a height watching them. Some had pitched
tents; others used lean-tos. The sun was about to set and a cold
west wind went whistling across the basin. Mercedes and I had
come up from Two Lakes after an afternoon of fishing. I came
empty handed, for my catch was all below the size limit. We had
come halfway when an Indian and his wife stopped their jeep
to give us a ride. In true Indian fashion the women took the rear
and I sat up front with this genial Yakima. When we reached the

basin and the blueberry encampment, he, learning I had no fish, endowed me with a half-dozen fourteen-inch eastern brook. Then an Indian woman stepped forward, called Mercedes by name, and put her arms around her.

"Myrtle Jim," Mercedes said, "what are you doing here?"

Myrtle Jim was once headed for a fine career in nursing when she suddenly quit.

"Why?" Mercedes asked.

Myrtle Jim pointed first to Mount Adams, now brilliant in the setting sun, and then to Potato Hill and the blueberry basin.

"This is my country. I could not stay away."

She said there were two times each year when the pull of the Cascades was too great to resist. One was August, when the blueberries ripened; the other was September, when the salmon started up the Columbia and all its tributaries.

"Then I must be with my people," Myrtle Jim said.

The night wind was picking up so much momentum that Myrtle Jim's tent cracked like a whip in the gusts that swept around it. The sun was almost off Mount Adams, and a chill settled over this blueberry basin. Myrtle Jim viewed the scene proudly.

"Look, how beautiful," she said. "And how much nicer than an apartment in Washington, D.C."

I knew what she meant, for Mount Adams, Potato Hill, Two Lakes, and all the other wonders of this high country also had a strange hold on me.

Bird Creek Meadows lies about a mile high on the southeast shoulder of Mount Adams. It's not a single meadow but a series of alcoves that run nearly a mile along the southern rim of the peak. And above each alcove is a series of benches, one higher than the other. Bird Creek is a stream so small at this point one can step across it. Alpine fir and white bark pine fringe these meadows. The highest bench above one of these meadows looks down on Hellroaring Creek and up at Mount Adams, which now seems so close as to be in touching distance. At this point I always feel as if I am standing on the threshold of another world. Mazama Glacier and Klickitat Glacier that feed Hellroaring Creek with milky water are dazzling in the brilliant July sun. Mount Adams is so high and massive it makes me shrink to the pint of ashes that man represents in the terrestrial scheme. The roar of the river comes faintly up the canyon. Above the roar can be heard the whine of the wind. All else is quiet. A golden eagle soars high in the void, catching a wind current. Nothing else moves.

Most glacial peaks exude an atmosphere of mystery. There is wonderment at the forces that created it. The sheer beauty of basalt cliffs, glacial ice, snow-crowned summits, and blue sky is tranquilizing. The clash and turmoil of civilization are far behind. Now one faces the elemental forces—those that produced the great mountain, those that are in process of leveling it. The Buddhist monasteries in Asia are usually built on sites which command great views. There is good reason for it. The wonders of nature lessen tensions and create relaxing moods. They seem to put one in touch with the infinite. All man-made sounds, all distractions, all complexities of life are left behind. Man on the edge of Bird Creek Meadows is alone with himself and with God. This is a place of wonderment and of worship. Men and their quarrels and jealousies are blown away into the void. The individual stands in awe before his Creator. The high meadow at Bird Creek is more wonderful than any man-made cathedral.

Bird Creek Meadows is a good starting point for a trip around

Mount Adams, going clockwise from south to west. There are lava beds to negotiate, ice-cold streams to cross, and ravines and ridges thick with trees to traverse. At the start Mount Adams looks down on the right, and across fertile fields and faraway ridges is Mount Hood on the left. After crossing Short Horn Creek the trail climbs a ridge; and now one has three snow-clad companions—Adams, Hood, and Saint Helens. Hood shortly is left behind; but before long Rainier looms up to the northwest and, shortly, the spectacular Goat Rocks. One of these four is now always in view; and sometimes all of them stand in splendor. No more scenic display exists in America.

This is the circle trip we like to take with our horses. My horse, King's X, is a sorrel with a white mark on his face that makes a perfect numeral one as written in Arabic. He is a quarter horse—gentle, sure-footed, well-mannered, and fast. King's X, one of the fastest walkers I have known, is not happy unless he is out front. Tumbleweed, brother to King's X, is Mercedes' horse; and he has mischief and curiosity added to his good manners. He is unhappy unless he is at the heels of King's X. Salah, the white Arabian, is Joni's pet. And Lady K—queen of all the Appaloosa—is for a guest. These four, plus pack horses, plus Sandy, the Shetland sheepdog who is everybody's friend, make up our party on the trip around Mount Adams.

As one moves south to west to north, he passes through meadow after meadow rich in bunch grass and gay in colors. Some are so thick with lupine and paintbrush that they are solid blue and cerise. Some meadows march almost to a glacier's edge; others are fringed at the upper end with trim alpine fir. Some meadows are bright with squaw grass. The delicate avalanche lily flourishes here as the snow recedes. Drier slopes are covered with mats of lavender and white phlox. The elk and deer tracks are fresh. Bobcats hightail it through tall timber. Ruffed grouse go out in large numbers underfoot. The mountain hemlock is on display on these western slopes, growing to great size and adding its tiny, lovely cones to the floor litter. Thick stands of white and red fir hung with yellow and black lichens cover some slopes. And in their deep shade the wild strawberries are in bloom.

The horses seem to love these meadows as much as we do. Cool streams make the sweet bunch grass luxuriant. Bird Creek Meadows, our starting point, holds horses for days on end. The other meadows, being smaller, make no such promise. But they, too, are minor horse heavens. Mad Cat Meadows, which lies just above Looking Glass Lake, is our first camp after leaving Bird Creek. These meadows have spring water so cold one can hardly hold it in his mouth. And the springs feed a creek where one can get his mess of brook trout in a few minutes before sunset. Mad Cat Meadows also boasts the largest, brightest yellow monkey flowers I have ever seen. For one addicted to unhurried travel this is a place to camp for days. The creek at Mad Cat Meadows and Looking Glass Lake are ideal fishing spots, and the surrounding woods are filled with deer, grouse, mushrooms, and wild flowers.

When I first traveled Mount Adams, as a boy, all its alpine meadows had pristine beauty. But today one who takes the circle trip finds at the northwest corner of the mountain exquisite meadows practically ruined by sheep. Dust has taken the place of bunch grass; pounding hoofs have torn up protective root systems; the slopes, heavy with the smell of sheep scat, promise to become an awful dust bowl, where spring runoffs create ugly gullies. This northwest corner is in the public domain. The north and east belong to the Indians, who exploit it greatly by allowing the white man to graze sheep and cattle there. Both areas are severely pounded, robbing this Mount Adams country, that was almost sacred to me, of much of its great glory.

A similar fate threatens Bird Creek Meadows. In the old days there were two routes there. A dirt road came up from the south to the base of Snowplow Mountain, where a trail (which a wagon could negotiate) took over. This old trail climbed steadily. High on a small bench is Mirror Lake, so marshy on the edges it is hard to find room to cast a fly. Above it about a mile is Bird Lake, a bright sapphire in a dark-green setting. It is a small lake, less than a hundred acres. It lies in a deep bowl just under Bird Creek Meadows to the north. Thick stands of balsam fir line it. Their shade was inviting to those of us who came on foot. And the small rainbow trout that filled the lake were delicious. This lake was so small and intimate it made an ideal camp for one party only. It was the place to stay for days, searching out beds of dainty phlox on the slopes above the lake, fishing from an old raft, or just lying on the shore watching fleecy clouds race by.

Another route to Bird Creek Meadows came from the west up Hellroaring Creek to Bench Lake. This lake lies about 4000 feet in a stand of Douglas fir and hemlock that produce deep shade for camping. When the ice first goes out, eastern brook trout make up most of the catch. Later the rainbow become active. Bench Lake is larger, less intimate, and less picturesque than Bird Lake. But for a man who has carried a pack from the valley it offers its own special rewards.

Whichever way we came, Bird Creek Meadows seemed a bit of paradise. Its alpine meadows are a mass of color during the first two months of summer. Great blankets of white and pink phlox cover the slopes. Spring beauty and monkey flowers decorate the creek. Indian paintbrush fills every field. There is purple fireweed too—fireweed that is knee-high. Pussypaws show streaks of white on the drier slopes—the plant whose tiny black seeds the chipmunks love. The more delicate alpine pussytoes are there too, making up extensive mats.

The Monterey mariposa nods gracefully in the creek bed, its lilac petals dainty and translucent in the bright sun. Ground damp from recent high water is thick with Honenmann's willow-herb that shows tiny purplish flowers. The tiny alpine speedwell turns whole hillsides azure blue. Streaks of a yellow hackweed cut through them.

I know of no alpine meadow more rewarding after a stiff climb. It is especially attractive on the bright days of July and August. Then the sky is a deep azure, the air cool and refreshing, Mount Adams splendid in its isolation. These high meadows even have charms when thunder echoes off the basalt cliffs of the mountain and the clouds close in. Then this high shoulder of the Cascades becomes a remote place, wrapped in fog and apart from this earth. The mist that settles down gives familiar objects a strange appearance; everything is blurred and out of focus. Mount Adams can produce weather peculiarly its own. While the sun is shining at Glenwood, the clouds around the mountain can spit sleet or spray ice-cold water. Local storms come and go during a night when no rain drops in the valley and he who planned to sleep out under the stars gets drenched.

I had not seen Bird Creek Meadows for over thirty years. I left Glenwood by jeep, planning to park it at road's end and hike in, as I used to do. As the jeep climbed on and on, I discovered to my dismay that the good dirt road went all the way. When I arrived, I counted twenty-seven cars ahead of me. My heart sank. An alpine meadow that I used to reach only after days of hiking was now accessible to everyone without effort. It had been desecrated by the automobile. This high shoulder of Mount Adams now had all the amenities of Rock Creek Park in Washington, D.C., and Central Park in New York City.

In the days that followed, I was greatly depressed by this transformation of Bird Creek Meadows. Potbellied men, smoking black cigars, who never could climb a hundred feet, were now in the sacred precincts of a great mountain. Part of the charm of Bird Creek Meadows had been their remoteness and the struggle to reach them. Their romantic nature had been diluted. The mountain was still as magnificent as ever; the sky as blue; the fireweed as brilliant. But the meadows were no longer a sanctuary. They had become merely another spot on a busy highway, where the quiet was broken by the roar of motors and the sound of spinning tires. People crowded here as they do at Coney Island. There was no escape for man. The auto was claiming even the remote refuges and converting them into public squares.

The loss of Bird Creek Meadows to the wilderness is symptomatic of the transformation going on in most of our far-western forest areas. I have seen in my lifetime a wilderness of trails remade into a maze of roads. There is hardly a place these days a jeep will not reach. The network of roads is so vast and intricate that almost every wilderness area is threatened. Along with the growing emphasis on roads has been a lack of attention to trails. Trails go unattended in the Mount Adams area year after year. Many have practically fallen into disuse. Local foresters deplore it. But there is little they can do. For Washington, D.C., decrees there shall be fewer and fewer funds for trail maintenance. Roads now claim the lion's share of the budget. And if the innermost thoughts of those in top command of our forests were known, they would probably reveal that the ultimate disaster is in the making—the substitution of roads for trails.

The road to Bird Creek Meadows is not explained by logging operations. It was the result of public pressure for a means of reaching the heights without effort. Yet most of the dirt roads in the Cascades are tied to lumbering. Ponderosa pine—the lumberman's prize tree that flourishes below 3000 feet on the eastern slopes of the Cascades—has been put on a selective cutting basis. Companies now operate on a permanent-yield basis, cutting ponderosa pine (and some white fir) in perpetuity. These forests are seldom clean-cut. Trees that are ripe, trees that are not thrift specimens, trees that are overage—these are the ones taken first. Under the system of selective cutting that is in vogue, the underbrush is piled and burned (in proper season) or broken up and plowed under. When I hike these areas where selective cutting takes place, a forest still remains. Yet the wilderness is gone. Logging trucks and jeeps roll by. There is no sense of isolation, of remoteness. Some values of the outdoors have been lost.

The destruction of wilderness is even more marked where clear cutting is done. Douglas fir cannot be cut on a selective basis. The stands are so thick and the trees so interdependent that if only some are cut the rest are apt to go down in the strong southwest winds that blow here. Moreover if only some are cut, their falling scrapes the bark off standing trees and makes those that are scarred very susceptible to fungi and other disease that infests these conifers. Finally, partial clearing of a Douglas fir forest makes reforestation difficult. For the remaining stands would be so thick as to make it difficult for young Douglas fir to get a foothold.

Douglas fir seed, like that of most conifers, has a wing which whirls the seed as it drops from the cone. This retards the fall, so that if there are any air currents, the seed will be carried away from the base of the parent tree. Instances have been known where these seeds have traveled several miles.

While the wind is a major element in transporting seed, the mice, chipmunks and squirrels play a part, though their role is secondary. With some trees, notably the juniper, birds help. But the Douglas fir seed loses viability when it passes through the alimentary canal of a bird.

Douglas fir that is clear-cut is reseeded by hand or machine. The reason is that natural reseeding might take twenty years or more. Douglas fir does not produce a good seed crop every year. Sometimes there is a cycle of four years or more when few seeds are produced. Meanwhile the clear-cut area grows up to brush. Then it, too, runs through a long cycle before Douglas fir seedlings can take hold.

The reseeding program that is introduced to avoid these consequences is varied. Seeds are more and more commonly sown by helicopter. There are methods of treating the seeds with poisons that will make them repellent to mice and other rodents. They may also be dipped in pigments to change their color and deceive the birds. Sometimes a whole area will first be poisoned, so as to eliminate the rodents before the reseeding takes place. While sowing by helicopter is taking the place of restocking by seedlings, many clear-cut areas are still planted with two-year-old seedlings grown in nurseries. Even then, difficult problems of regeneration remain. The new, open areas where the seedlings are planted are attractive to many plants that would not grow in the deep shade of a Douglas fir forest. These young plants produce browse that the deer love. Succulent plants for rabbits also flourish here. The invasion of deer and rabbits has serious consequences, for they eat the young Douglas fir seedlings, topping them and retarding their growth. And so the search goes on for a chemical that will impart impalatability to the young tree itself. To date, experts have succeeded in making the Douglas fir seedlings immune from rabbit attack for seventeen months.

The young Douglas fir trees also have an enemy in the bear. The bears sit on the ground, wrap their forelegs around a small fir, and chew the bark, girdling the tree and causing it to die. By the early '50s it was estimated that in Washington the bears were destroying up to 90 per cent of the young trees. One bear could chew as many as forty young firs a day. The reasons the bears became so destructive were twofold. First, the bear population had greatly increased in the Pacific Northwest and their need for food had multiplied. Second, the bark on the old trees was too thick for bears to strip. The appearance of new, open areas where the young seedlings were planted produced berries and grasses which made them ideal feeding grounds for bears. Bears therefore congregated in these regions where tree farms were located. The bear population on the feeding grounds exceeded the normal food supply. So the animals turned to the sweet cambium layer beneath the bark of the Douglas fir. Lumber companies stepped up their program for hunting the bear; and in the late '50s the bear kill in Washington alone ran from 5000 to 7000 a year. But scientists think they have an additional answer. They are working on a chemical that will so change the flavor of the sap of the Douglas fir that the bears will pass by those trees!

While clear-cutting creates great problems, it is being used successfully to put the cutting of Douglas fir on a perpetual basis, the cycle being somewhere between eighty and 150 years, depending on local conditions. One of the most advanced programs of this kind (described in Stevens' *Green Power*) is on the west side of the Cascades near Shelton, Washington, where nearly 300,000 acres of private and public land in Douglas fir are being cut on a perpetual-yield basis. This program has saved two communities from extinction and has put several thousand workers into permanent jobs. That program was executed under the authority of the act of March 29, 1944, which authorizes, subject to certain controls, federal forest lands to be pooled with private forest lands for cutting and management on a sustained-yield basis. This contract for the Shelton area is made with a private lumber operator for a 100-year term. The agreement provides that the cutting must be based on sound forestry standards; that the timber must be manufactured locally; that wood waste must be held to the minimum; that the selling price of the federally owned timber must be reviewed periodically and revised upward or downward, according to market conditions.

That kind of program for perpetual cutting will expand more and more into our public lands as our population increases and as the demand for lumber mounts. It will include not only ponderosa pine and Douglas fir but other trees as well. About 16 per cent of the nation's commercial timberland (exclusive of Alaska and Puerto Rico) is in national forests. These public holdings contain twice as much saw timber per acre as the average of all private commercial lands. As the nation grows, the pressures to reach into our national forests and parks for commercial operation will increase. This is inevitable. The practice of putting ponderosa pine and Douglas fir on cycles of cuttings will spread.

But as that goes forward, the need to preserve wilderness areas will likewise mount. Man must be able to escape civilization if he is to survive. Some of his greatest needs are for refuges and retreats where he can recapture for a day or a week the primitive conditions of life.

There are ridges, basins, and meadows in the Cascade region that have some merchantable timber but which never could be put on a sustained-yield basis. Their main value is aesthetic. The few ponderosa pine or Douglas fir that stand there are pillars in a cathedral. A road to reach them would turn a place of beauty into a bald, devastated, ugly place. The road—on whose construction the logger often makes a greater profit than he does on the timber he takes out—would be a road to nowhere. For with the forest removed, the place has become a ridge or basin of desolation. Even the game has gone; there is nothing to see. The road becomes a watercourse for the spring runoff.

The loggers and road builders look at every lovely ridge or basin for quick profits. They take heavily from the forests, sometimes destroying everything. There are others who take nothing from the forest except inspiration and high purpose. Their lives and character are indeed shaped by it.

Mercedes and I talked of those things as we followed in swirling dust twenty-seven cars down the road from Bird Creek Meadows. "Surely," I said, "those who look at towering pines and firs only with wonderment and walk trails with no thought of profit should not be forgotten in the mad rush to build roads everywhere."

That night I made some computations. Only two per cent or so of our land area remains in a roadless, wilderness state. Most of this is in the public domain—parts of national forests, national parks, wildlife refuges, and Indian reservations. It is roughly estimated at 55 million acres, which, divided up among all our people, averages about one-third acre each. The residue of wildness in America has reached a minimum which all who love trails and peaks must now defend.

I realized from my day's journey how badly we need high alpine meadows which can only be reached on foot, how badly we need peaks which can only be conquered by daring. The passion to bring "civilization" into our wilderness areas is one sign that we Americans are getting soft and flabby. We want everything made easy. Yet success is worth having only when it comes through great effort and hazardous exertion.

The logistics of abundance call for mass production. This means the ascendency of the machine. The risk of man's becoming subservient to it are great. The struggle of our time is to maintain an economy of plenty and yet keep man's freedom intact. Roadless areas are one pledge to freedom. With them intact, man need not become an automaton. There he can escape the machine and become once more a vital individual. If these inner sanctuaries are invaded by the machine, there is no escape. For men and civilization will be molded by mass compulsions. If our wilderness areas are preserved, every person will have a better chance to maintain his freedom by allowing his idiosyncracies to flower under the influence of the wonders of the wilderness.

These were my thoughts that night as I sat on my lawn watching the last glow of the sun leave the high snow fields of Mount Adams.

CHAPTER VI

OLYMPIC MOUNTAINS

THE Olympics—that loom up from Puget Sound as jagged peaks against the western sky—are low, as mountains go. Of the twenty-odd major peaks there is none over 8000 feet. Only six are over 7000 feet, Mount Olympus rising 7954 feet. Yet no American range has more interesting features. The rain forests near the base are botanical wonders. Above them are alpine meadows and peaks that offer challenges. At least fifty living glaciers flank these peaks, three on Mount Olympus being two miles or more in length.

The work of the ice age is evident on every hand. Great cirques mark the heads of most valleys. Deep blue lakes lie above moraines. The peaks are highly polished. There are few rounded domes, most of the peaks being sharp and pointed. Many ridges are razor-edged.

The Olympics are sandstone, shale, and lava. During four successive periods—each separated by millions of years—the site of this range was covered by the sea. Each period of inundation was followed by an uplift. The first three uplifts were reduced by erosions to nearly sea level. The fourth uplift was also followed by erosion, which removed thousands of feet of sediment, leaving stubs of mountains. Once again parts of the area were inundated. Then came the great geologic period of mountain building—between one and eleven million years ago. That was the date of the fifth uplift of the Olympics, which took place when the Alps, Andes, Cascades, and Himalaya were being created.

Peaks that have come and gone four times should halt a man in his steps.

The rivers that run off the western slopes of the Olympics are among our shortest. The Quillayute, Hoh, and Quinault are not much more than fifty miles long, and their water is as clean as the rain and snow that feed them, save for the glacial "flour" that at times discolors them. Their run to the Pacific is through land as close to the jungle as the Temperate Zone has created. The west and south watersheds have rainfall that averages in the lower reaches about twelve inches a month. Higher up there has sometimes been twenty inches a month. The result is a mass of vegetation so thick that the newcomer will think it impenetrable.

Salmon and steelhead run these streams in the Fall and Winter, cutthroat trout in the Summer. The Quinault Indians use canoes, hewn by hand out of cedar logs. Memories of my hours with them on fast waters, fishing for cutthroat, are bright. There are pools where one can hold a canoe for several casts with a fly. But in most places the water of the Quinault is too swift for that. One cast at the point of a log, one on the edge of white water below a swirl, one in an opening left by vine maple that partially covers flat water, one where a graceful red alder touches a pool. One cast, a wait of a split second while the fly drifts and the canoe shoots on. Almost before the fly can be retrieved the canoe is above another spot. The timing must be perfect, the cast must bring the fly down softly, the reprieve must be quick. This is exquisite fishing. Chances are won or lost in a split second.

The miles run off in rapid fashion in these fast waters; the cinema of white, roaring whirlpools, boulders barely missed, fast runs under alder, swirling eddies around logs make me lose all sense of time. Strange as it may seem, there is no letdown, no sense of frustration if I return empty handed. A morning on one of those fast streams brings joy and excitement enough.

One who runs these rivers has the sense of being primitive man pitted against the elements. His skills, his endurance are all that count. There is no community to underwrite his errors, to make up for his mistakes. All that matters is his skill, and his alone.

A rowboat takes one down leisurely. By August the water is down and spits of white sand, ideal for sun bathing, are exposed. The woods by then are fairly dry; red alders offer shade and thick ferns make a restful bed for an afternoon siesta.

The slow drift by boat offers a deep solitude, unbroken except for the sound of rushing water, the splash of a muskrat, or the song of a water ouzel. The wilderness presses in on all sides and shuts out the world of man. The roar of civilization is left behind. I like to hold the boat against the side of the pool and watch the river life go by. Hellgrammites and periwinkles are in the gravel. A crayfish moves cautiously. A frog is spread out as if relaxed. Swarms of small fish, hatched on nearby spawning grounds, race by. Some of these fingerlings are steelhead who stay in the river two winters before moving to the sea. Full-grown cutthroat are deep in the pool—poised, alert, intent. A salmon weighing thirty pounds or more—probably a jack—heads upstream. A stray steelhead streaks across the pool.

There are swifts along the river and hummingbirds too. The western belted kingfisher is busy. A little flycatcher with grayish body and yellow belly calls "swit-zo, swit-zo" from the alders. The chickadee calls over and over from the brush. The brilliant western tanager, high in the alders, shouts "petik, petik."

By June the elk are in alpine meadows. There are deer where there is browse; and these black-tailed deer love the river bottoms. The bear are numerous. I remember one bright August day when August Slathar had the oars, holding the middle of the Bogachiel on a long, slow drift in flat water as I whipped the river with a fly. As we rounded a bend, we saw a large black bear on the next point, a couple of hundred yards distant. Augie gave me a knowing look and pointed the boat directly to the animal. The wind was right and, as fortune would have it, the rear end of the bear was pointed our way. He had flipped a big fish from the water and was leisurely engaged in eating it. When the boat was within three feet of the bear, I reached over and gave it a slap on the back, shouting, "What are you doing here?"

It was seconds before the message reached the bear's brain. Meanwhile his sympathetic nervous system went into operation. His rear legs visibly stiffened; his back seemed to freeze. Then the danger signal reached consciousness and the animal was off through the dense brush, not once looking behind.

Winter fishing on these streams offers different rewards. Rain brings the water level up as much as eleven feet. The pools are still there, although there are few old landmarks to identify them.

The sooty or blue grouse have come down from the mountains. The loons have arrived from the north. So have the Oregon juncos. Geese and ducks are in migration, and if one is lucky he'll see a veritable armada of whistling swan flying south in a single line that is several city blocks long. If one looks closely, he may see a pygmy owl sitting on an old snag.

The days are dark, foggy, and cold. Ice forms on the ferrules of the fishing rod. The chill in the air strikes into the marrow. These are the days when the steelhead come upstream. They have good cover under the flood waters.

Sandy Balcom—best of all steelheaders—is my mentor. We try to hold a boat above a pool and to fish it according to its peculiar hydraulics. We try to cast so that the current at the head of the pool will take the bait in a long arc to the far end. The theory is that a steelhead lies in wait there for food that the river brings down. Frequently the theory works. The strike may be a ferocious taking, or it may be only the gentlest of touches. Once the hook is set, a battle royal begins, and numb fingers are forgotten. The fish may circle the pool several times, breaking water and shaking its head to get rid of the hook. Before long it heads downstream and makes the reel fairly sing.

Not all winter days are alike. Once there was no rain for a month and the temperature was so low that no snow was melting. Sandy Balcom and I had to drag our boat over gravel from pool to pool. The sun was out, the day bright. The low water made every steelhead unusually wary. Our dream of hooking 25-pound steelheads—about the largest in these streams—vanished. By noon we were ready to settle for much less. By mid-afternoon we would have been happy with cutthroat. By late afternoon we had about given up hope. We had drifted twelve miles without a strike. When we came to an old, abandoned farm, we beached the boat and walked downstream to fish two pools shaded by a western hemlock and heavily guarded by thick stands of salal. Before we made the first cast a dark cloud drifted in from the Pacific, shutting out the sun. In less than three minutes Sandy and I were each playing steelheads—twins that weighed six pounds each.

As we dressed the fish, the silence of this wilderness closed in. Though we were only a mile or so from my fishing lodge, the distance from civilization seemed great. The trees and brush formed a tangled jungle on each side of the river and towered over us. The river was our one path home. Now a cold, soft rain began to fall and the dense woods set up a dripping that would last for days.

The lower reaches of the Olympics have many small bogs, ponds, or lakes a few acres in size, formed in the glacial period. Some are true sphagnum bogs. James Lake has not quite reached that stage, though it is on its way. It is only a mile or so from my fishing lodge and has supplied me with an interesting listening point. The short walk there is an experience. I always go cross-country under the dark canopy of western hemlock and spruce. There is a tangle of brush, ferns, and down timber. I climb over logs that are eight feet or more in diameter and make my way through thick salal brush. James Lake is a small target—only a few acres in size and easy to miss. I wait some minutes before stepping out of the jungle, so as not to disturb any animals that may be there. This is a quiet alcove to approach reverently. It is a sanctuary where voices above a whisper seem almost sacrilegious. Here I remember Thoreau's words, "I enter a swamp as a sacred place." A hemlock fell decades ago and now lies partly above the water. Its bark is gone, and its wood, worn by weather into long grooves, is decorated with moss and lichens. Beside it grow swamp laurel, Labrador tea, and northern cranberry. It is here I like to stretch out on a summer day. A biologist lying on my log will see life without end in the shallow, darkish water. A botanist, too, will find adventure here.

The bog myrtle and crabapple get their feet wet along the shore line. So does the cascara. The Douglas spirea flourishes here. The surrounding woods, made up mostly of western hemlock and red cedar, put up a thick green wall around this placid lake. Its waters are dark blue against a somber green setting. Lily pads show white and yellow blossoms throughout the season. There are gentians, northern starflowers and violets along the edges of the log. The far shore shows cotton grass. A wood duck (green head, red chest, and buff-colored sides) lands to cruise the opposite shore. A colony of muskrat is busy. A doe steps into the open, her big ears flicking. A bumblebee breaks the silence; a Virginia rail makes an excited call. To my left there is the sound of a stick quickly cracked. The noise is as sharp as a rifle shot. A huge bear, dark brown in color, comes to the edge of the lake. He does not see me nor pick up my scent. He sits down on a log, his back to me, and starts scooping off salmonberries. He has nearly had his fill when I raise myself slightly and cough. The echo comes back from the opposite shore, but not before the doe has lifted her head and stiffened. The wood duck, too, takes notice by changing its direction and picking up speed. A muskrat crossing a nearby log freezes in his tracks. A frog jumps off the lily pad. The bear jumps as if hit by buckshot and bolts into the woods. He crashes through thick stands of brush, putting everything out of the way. He does not stop running for several hundred yards, while the noise of his hurried exit fills the place.

James Lake changes with the seasons. Summer finds it low. The fall rains raise its level. The first snows on the high slopes of the Olympics cause the elk to start down. By late October they are in the woods around James Lake. One who lies on my log at dawn or dusk at that time can count herds up to sixty that come there to browse and to drink.

When I paddle a canoe through the north country of Minnesota or fish the high lakes of Oregon or Washington, those waters seem permanent and enduring. But James Lake teaches the lesson that lakes, too, must pass. Like other life, lakes are in transition. They gradually fill up, form sphagnum and peat bogs, collect all the debris that rains wash in and that vegetable growth produces. Before long they are dry and reclaimed by the forests.

Another hold the Olympics has on me comes from the rain forests. Of the several rain forests the one to my liking is on the Hoh River. The zone that lies in the Hoh Valley below 1000 feet is as interesting and unique as any segment of our forests the nation over.

One who comes from the ocean front passes through a spruce-cedar climax forest. This lies below the 1000-foot level and is made up of the Sitka spruce, red cedar, and western hemlock. The rain forest is farther inland. Each rain forest has a bottom carved out by a glacier. The valley is not a mile wide in places and runs on average fourteen miles in length within park boundaries. The stream gradients are very gradual. Yet in spite of this and the heavy rainfall, the valley floors—consisting of glacial till and water-deposited sands and gravel—are well drained, little standing water being in evidence even after the heaviest rain.

Sitka spruce is dominant in the rain forest, some of them 300 feet high and over ten feet in diameter. Western hemlock, which rises up to 200 feet high, comes next among the conifers, and the red cedar last. Douglas fir is here too. Douglas fir, which occasionally reaches 300 feet, is what the foresters call a pioneer species. It comes in whenever the mineral soil is bared, as after a heavy windfall or fire. Since Douglas fir cannot reproduce in shade, the western hemlock and red cedar eventually take over. That process, continued indefinitely, would eliminate the Douglas fir from the Pacific Northwest forests. Something, however, is always happening that clears the thick woods and opens them up. When that occurs, Douglas fir manages to hold its own.

The Sitka spruce dominate the rain forest today. The branches and leaves of these high trees form a roof that lets in only shafts of sunlight. The understory is big leaf maple, vine maple, devil's club. Down logs are covered with a thick carpet of mosses. Sometimes they are so completely covered by moss and so heavy with young growth that they look like a low hedge. The trees are hung with mosses, liverworts, and lichens that cover the trunks and even the crowns. These are the epiphytes that have no connection with the soil. They get their nutrients from rain water, windborne particles, and the decaying bark of their host. They are not parasites but rather hitchhikers of the rain forest. Underfoot are bracken and other ferns, the bead-ruby with glossy leaves, wood sorrel, wild strawberries, red huckleberries, Oregon grape, and fragrant bed-straw. There are snails and millipedes in the moss. Some lichens are coral colored with brilliant red tips. Some are shaped like cups and painted orange.

Due to the extreme wetness of the forest, the down logs are

ancient relics. Decomposition is so slow that some have lain there for 400 years. They often have tiny rows of Sitka spruce on them, seedlings not more than a few inches high. The seeds that fall on the damp ground, heavy with moss, ferns, and grass, have little chance for survival. Those that land on the old log have head room to grow and lesser competition. This old log will be a nurse to the seedlings for many years. In time they will send their roots down and around the nurse log to the ground. For some years the new trees will appear to be standing on stilts. But in time—perhaps several hundred years later—the nurse log will have decomposed, much of it being absorbed by the new trees. Then the roots will enlarge and fill up the space left by the nurse log. Those that travel the forest on that future day will see giants where I saw seedlings. Not knowing about the old nurse log, they may wonder why it is that these new trees are swollen, distorted, and heavily buttressed at the base. And they may also wonder why the trees stand in a row, giving a colonnade effect.

Loggers often claim that overage trees and down trees are wasted and should be removed. That is a false premise in the Olympics. For in the true rain forest these rotting logs are the best seed ground available.

Thanks to the elk, the forest floor is fairly free of thick underbrush; one can see for some distance.

On a rainy day the force of the storm is broken by the treetops. Only a slight drizzle comes through. After a hard rain the trees will drip for days. On a bright day the shafts of sunlight fill the rain forest with a soft green light that is restful to the eyes. Rain or shine, this forest has a quiet that is deep and profound. A winter wren sings high overhead. Though few birds are seen in the rain forest, many breed there—ruffed grouse, jays, tanagers, grosbeaks, finches, siskins, juncos, warblers, and song sparrows.

A snowshoe rabbit runs underfoot. A Douglas squirrel sounds the alarm. Every noise is soft and muted. The quiet and the light induce a mood of reverence. This is not a place to run, to shout. This is a cathedral, draped in mosses and lichens and made of gigantic trees. The trees alone are enough to bring humility to man. The western hemlock is over twenty-five feet in girth, Douglas fir over fifty feet, and Sitka spruce over forty feet. These are virgin trees in a virgin forest. They would have disappeared by now if the logging interests had had their way. There are some who see in them no more than so many board feet. But they are among the great wonders of creation. Kellogg bluegrass and the delicate trefoil foam flower flourish near the trail in the rain forest. The trailing raspberry with its starry five-petaled white flowers is bright. The showy miner's lettuce, with white petals, makes a thick stand. The waxen white wintergreen and the rose-colored Oregon oxalis sorrel are almost hidden in the litter of the forest floor. The snowberry—later to have white fruit—shows pink flowers. Everywhere stands the graceful vanilla leaf, its slender cluster of white flowers high on a single stem rising above one leaf divided into three broad leaflets.

There are fungi in every forest and every field. But I never feel their presence so vividly as I do in the rain forest. Here are molds, mildew, mushrooms, shelf fungus, rust, to mention only a few. Thousands of others work unseen in the vegetation that makes a soft, thick carpet underfoot. Some produce spores that fill the air and cause people to suffer from allergies. But all of them perform functions crucially essential to forests and fields.

Forest humus is not a mass of plant remains but a living mass of fungi. The genera alone run into the thousands. Bacteria predominate in soil rich in nutrients, cultivated, and fertilized. Fungi are more active in the forests and in compact, poor soils. They are present even in nearly pure silicious sands.

Since the fungi have no chlorophyll, they lack the means of manufacturing their own food. They must, therefore, be parasites and live on other living things, or be saprophytes, or scavengers, and live on dead organic matter. They do one or the other, most of them being saprophytic. The latter have a far wider range of food than the parasites.

Parasites do not live on vegetation alone. Some live on microscopic animals, insects, worms, fluke eggs, and the larvae of mosquitoes.

While some saprophytes are scavengers of vegetable matter, others consume carcasses of animals, some live on animal excrement, and so on. Each supply of organic material seems to have its special saprophyte.

Dozens of strains of fungi have been shown to be capable of inhibiting the growth of bacteria and of producing a variety of antibiotic substances. Some fungi destroy other fungi that are parasitic, and bacteria as well.

Soil-inhabiting fungi produce organic acids which dissolve inorganic soil elements such as calcium, magnesium, and phosphorus and make them available for food. Sometimes this food, produced by the fungi, is used by them. Most of it, however, is used by green plants. The decomposed materials, not eaten by the fungi or used by green plants, are left as humus. Humus is resistant to rapid attack by micro-organisms and forms a cohesive part of the soil system. These soil fungi—whether in forests or fields—are, therefore, highly important to soil fertility.

The logs at my feet in the Olympics have been collecting spores of fungi from the time the trees fell. Only those spores which can use this particular wood will flourish on this down timber. Some fungi feed on hardwoods, some on conifers, some on leaves. Each has its special diet. One set of fungi may cause the primary decay in the logs; another set may come in later and attack the remains. Some fungi, such as the coral mushroom, are parasitic on the roots of trees. Poking my foot into the litter of the forest floor, I turn up a small colony of mushrooms, *Agaricus subrutilescens*. These tender morsels, low to the ground and shaped like a Japanese parasol, are delicious when broiled in butter. They are one of many mushrooms that flourish in the dark, damp wood of the rain forest. And when we pick them it has no more effect on the mushroom plant than picking fruit from a tree. What we pick is the fruit. The plant is a vast network of threads so fine that they are not visible to the naked eye until they are twisted into strands. These threads produce enzymes which digest food particles outside the threads. When the digested material is in solution, and only then, is it absorbed by the plant. The spores from this dainty mushroom at my feet will spread; but the plant will produce mushrooms over and again. If I can only mark this spot, I will find, on my return after more warm rains, a new crop from the old plant.

I learned in the Olympics an important lesson in ecology. The lesson is that wilderness areas are essential to our long-time welfare and well-being as a nation. The wilderness area is the norm. In the areas where man has introduced crops, sprays, fertilizers, the ecological balance has been upset. At times the result may be harmful. DDT can make milk from cows dangerous to humans. Certain fruit sprays kill bees that are essential to pollenization. At other times the remedy used by man merely helps nature in her corrective process. Yet the wilderness stands as the true "control" plot for all experimentation in the animal and vegetable worlds. Only through knowledge of the norm can an appraisal

of the abnormal or diseased be made. The "control" plot, where vegetable and animal growth continues undisturbed, is as essential to successful diagnosis and management of soil conditions as normal individuals are to the practice of medicine.

That is, I think, what Thoreau meant when he wrote, "In wildness is the preservation of the world." Farming, for example, imports plants, animals, and fertilizers. It eliminates native flora and fauna and even some of the unseen fungi and bacteria that have built the soil. All this is necessary for human existence. But will it stabilize the soil or will we end with sterile land and ugly gullies? No one knows. Nature got stability by encouraging great diversity. We do not yet know whether we can do the same through man-made substitutes.

No species should ever be eliminated, for man in his wisdom does not yet know the full wonders and details of the cosmic scheme.

On one side lichens, fungi, insects, bacteria, mammals, birds, and on the other the trees, ferns, and underbrush are interlocked or combined into a community in this Olympic forest. It is a community of competition and of interdependence. It is a series of food chains too intricate for man to comprehend in all its ramifications.

The rain forests are so radiant with soft green light, so filled with endless wonders that I hate to leave them. Yet when I reach the high ridges and meadows of the Olympics I hate to leave them also.

There are many paths that lead to the summits. My favorite is Graves Creek, one of the tributaries of the Quinault. From road's end it is only twelve miles to the Enchanted Valley, and in that distance one gains only a few hundred feet in elevation. The trail is fine for horses, and there are lush meadows at the head of the canyon where they can graze. Yet one should take this trip only on foot.

That is the way Daniel B. Beard, of the Park Service, Elon Gilbert, and I reached the Enchanted Valley. Dan was born to the woods and is a naturalist of distinction. To Elon any stretch of woods is a sanctuary. So as we hiked we had keen, observing, understanding eyes absorbing even the minutiae.

This is ground to explore closely. Even when travel is slow it would take repeated journeys to see only a part of the wonders. There are small streams every quarter mile or so, and their water seems sweeter to the taste than any I know. After the rain forest proper has been left behind, the ground is still thick with moss. Big-leafed maples now appear in open orchards, every bit of them from trunk to crown hung with thick mats of bright green moss. On the river flats the red alder grows in spectacular stands. They seldom stand straight; yet, unlike trees in wind-blown areas, they do not lean one way. They are gracefully arranged to make every grove an artistic creation. And the higher one goes the lighter the bark, until in some places it seems that this is a bit of the birch forests of the northland transplanted.

The western hemlock marches most of the way to the En- chanted Valley. And its cones—the smallest of any of our western conifers—literally cover sections of the trail, making the under- footing soft and springy.

If the fireweed is at its peak in the lower valley, the trail along Graves Creek is almost certain to be lined for miles and miles with the Siberian miner's lettuce. The dainty pinkish flowers stand gracefully on slender stalks growing out of two broad basal leaves. The plant is succulent, as good as lettuce. The trefoil foam flower, with tiny white lacelike flowers, is second in abundance. Occasional stands of the monkey flower show bright yellow.

Cinquefoil shows an even deeper yellow. Delicate white hawk-weeds grow in the damper places. The tiny American speedwell adds touches of blue. Purple self-heal (whose juice the Indians mixed with grease to make an ointment) are common. Bleeding hearts are abundant. The low bunchberry dogwood is nearly gone. The bloom of the oxalis has passed, but its shamrock-shaped leaves cover the shaded ground. The vanilla leaf is in seed. Some blackberries are still in bloom. The thimbleberries are beginning to ripen, and the red huckleberry too.

Along the river bank are water ouzels, flitting from rock to rock looking for beetles in the moss and periwinkles in the water. Somewhere high in the trees is the tiny western winter wren, who serenades the traveler all the way to the Enchanted Valley.

The eastern canyon wall at Enchanted Valley is almost sheer. It is an imposing precipice, adorned by rugged escarpments and ledges without number. This wall spouts several dozen waterfalls in July. Some will last all Summer, for they are fed by large pockets of perpetual snow. These waterfalls that drop 2000 feet or so fill the deep, narrow valley with music that can be heard above the murmur of Graves Creek. This eastern wall is a spectacle at the close of day. The sun leaves the bottom of the canyon early and sends a shadow up the eastern wall, turning it into a sundial. And in the morning the shadow creeps slowly downward on the opposite wall. Morning or night is the time to watch this steep eastern wall for mountain goat. Though the cliffs seem sheer, there are pockets of meadows among them. Here the goats feed, though it may take field glasses to detect them.

At the head of this canyon is Anderson Peak (7365 feet), which shows Hanging Glacier on its south slopes. This glacier used to move downward until it hung over the edge of the canyon wall. Then it would break into huge ice blocks with a roar that would fill the Enchanted Valley. These Olympic glaciers, like others of the Pacific Northwest, are the habitat of the snow or ice worms—species of the genus *Mesenchytraeus*. They are black and an inch long. Their activity picks up with the melting snow. But they die when removed and exposed to normal temperature. The birds of the Olympics feast on them. Hanging Glacier these days is receding. It is an invitation to those who have crampons, rope, and ice axes. One crosses it when he climbs Anderson Peak. But there is a trail that swings west and south of Anderson and climbs the western wall above the Enchanted Valley and takes one to Hart Lake and LaCrosse Lake—two alpine gems of the Olympics.

At about 4000 feet the western hemlock is supplanted by the mountain hemlock, every cone of which is a miniature tree, perfectly formed. Now the Pacific silver fir and the peaked alpine fir take over. Mountain ash begins to appear, along with a few Alaska yellow cedars. The Hart Lake trail is mostly in shade all the way to the top, except where it crosses alpine meadows. In July the elderberry bush is in bloom at these altitudes. The pioneer violet shows dainty yellow flowers. A few queencup bead-lily are beginning to show their dainty white petals between two glossy leaves. In open areas the tiny purple alpine speedwell is in bloom. Shooting stars show purplish pink in shady spots. The Alaska spirea is much in evidence. Mountain dandelions are on display. Marsh marigolds—white petals with yellow centers—seem to be rushing into bloom on warm hillsides. A few clumps of squaw grass show their creamy white blossoms. Some delicate western pasqueflowers, whose dainty plumes appear in August, are beginning to bloom in mid-July. A tiny alpine buttercup is gay. The alpine meadows have just been rid of their thick snow blankets. The alpine fir has hardly yet recovered from the great weight that was on it for months. Sedges that will grow eighteen inches high are begining to reach upward. Lupine is not yet in bloom. Only a few blossoms of the low-bush blueberry and the thickly matted white-flowered cassiope are out. False hellebore is fresh and thick but yet to blossom. The alpine meadows are on the edge of a great awakening that will transform them. What gives them their greatest distinction this day is the avalanche lily. This delicate flower with white petals and yellow centers comes up on the very edge of snowbanks and follows the snow as it retreats. Mid-July, Dan Beard, Elon Gilbert, and I found acres of them on the high slopes along the trail to Hart Lake. We sat in the shade of mountain hemlock, admiring them. Three bull elk in turn watched us and then stepped behind a clump of alpine fir and hurriedly crossed several snow fields. A Pacific varied thrush called over and again. A ruffed grouse set up his drumming in the thick forest below us.

The snow fields on these high Olympic ridges will not be gone until August first. Shortly Fall will set in. There will be five feet of snow or more in the Enchanted Valley before many months pass. On the high ridge where we sit the drifts will be many times that deep. In the short interval between now and then the canyon walls of the Enchanted Valley will be ablaze with colors.

Life comes quickly and passes quickly on these Olympic ridges. Those who have the urge to turn their backs on cities and seek the glories of high alpine meadows have only a few precious weeks for their adventure.

CHAPTER VII

GOOSE PRAIRIE

IN his book, *Travels with a Donkey*, Robert Louis Stevenson tells of a delightful night among the pines where "the room was airy, the water excellent, and the dawn had called me to a moment." Feeling indebted for "this liberal entertainment" that the wildness had accorded him, he thought he should somehow compensate for it. "And so it pleased me, in a half-laughing way, to leave pieces of money on the turf as I went along, until I had left enough for my night's lodging. I trust they did not fall to some rich and churlish drover."

I feel that way whenever I stay at Goose Prairie. When I first knew the place, I went by foot some forty miles. I knew it as a boy when a rutted dirt road, servicing a new reclamation dam on Bumping Lake, reached it. The lake is on the east side of the Cascades, right under the divide. Goose Prairie, which is short of the lake, is a mountain meadow of a few hundred acres that is rimmed by steep slopes thick with conifers. Here is found the greatest variety of conifers of any place in our entire country. Goose Prairie even boasts yew trees.

Tom Fife, who homesteaded it, had a log cabin there. I knew Tom when I was a boy. His cabin had a door facing the trail, and it was always open to travelers. Tom, a refugee from the coal mines of Pennsylvania, found heaven at Goose Prairie. The air was pure and fresh; rainbow were in the river; Scotch bluebells reigned supreme in the meadows. Tom always kept a pot of beans in the fireplace where he did his cooking, and if a visitor gave him a few hours, he could make a delicious mulligan of red squirrels.

Goose Prairie also meant warmhearted Jack Nelson, who, when I first back-packed into that country, was the lock tender at the dam on Bumping Lake. Jack and his wife, Kitty, took me in out of many a storm, warmed me with hot coffee and soup, and helped me see and understand some of the wonders of this piece of wildness. Today there is a paved road to Goose Prairie, a fourth-class post office, a permanent Boy Scout camp, Double K Mountain Ranch, and a few summer homes. Since I found kindness and hospitality deep in these woods, I have long loved Goose Prairie. I also love it for the natural wonders on display and for the back country it commands.

I knew Goose Prairie in Winter, Fall, and Summer. I have seen it heavy with snow streaked with snow lice that come in after storms and furnish the chickadees with a feast. In the Winter a deep silence comes to Goose Prairie and settles over the woods. I have walked it with snowshoes and seen elk traveling up to their shoulders in runways that lead to stands of willow and alder, on which they browse. When the willow and alder give out, the elk turn to lichen that hangs like beards from the conifers. One is bright yellow (*Litharia vulpina*), one is blackish (*Alectoria fremontii*), and one is sea-green (*Alectoria sarmentosa*). Some Winters it is the lichen that pulls the elk through. Hunger is not the only enemy that stalks the elk—and the deer too. Lynx, bob-cat, and coyote also winter at Goose Prairie.

Summers at Goose Prairie are gentle. Jack Nelson, who has now spent nearly fifty years there, Catherine Clark, a botanist, and Kay Kershaw, who runs the guest ranch known as Double K, have found in it over 400 species of wild flowers. Grass grows knee-high, and the wild flowers that are lush and brilliant send streaks of color through it. I love Goose Prairie especially for the vanilla leaf that shows a cluster of white flowers high on a stem above a leaf divided into three broad leaflets. There are rainbow trout in Bumping River, and I wrap my fish in this slightly scented plant.

Goose Prairie is the home of many birds. Jack Nelson has personally known over seventy species that frequent this valley. In Winter I have seen the water ouzel teetering on icy boulders in the Bumping River, singing its heart out. Muir said that the water ouzel "sings deliciously all winter," that it "makes a summer any time of the year." It certainly brightens the winter hours at Goose Prairie. Clarke's crow—with black tail and wings, fringed with white, and gray body—is on hand, scolding for crumbs. Once I almost stepped on the white-tailed ptarmigan, perfectly camouflaged in this white-black setting. The Oregon jay, or camp robber, will land on one's hat or shoulder for food. The Steller's jay—cobalt blue with black head and crest—scolds loudly on frosty days. Red-shafted flickers winter at Goose Prairie. The rosy-red finch is a regular winter visitor that searches the bark of dead logs for insects. Pinedrops—the strange plant that grows four feet tall and produces a host of white flowers on a stalk that is covered with sticky hairs—often sticks up above the snow. Now it is a dry, bronze stalk decorated with pretty seed vessels that the birds like. The horned owl makes his presence known all Winter long. From a perch high in a Douglas fir, the blue or sooty grouse gives a muffled hooting that breaks the stillness of a winter day. Franklin's grouse—the famous fool hen of the west— is also present. This bird, whose red brows often meet on the top of its head, has a friendly curiosity, making it easy to approach. Its apparent lack of fear has done much to lessen its numbers. They are not heard in Winter and seldom seen. They huddle in the fir trees, well camouflaged and living on the needles. The ruffed grouse is more conspicuous. He beds down in fresh snow and often flies up under one's snowshoes. Come March, the ruffed grouse sits on a log, drumming. The sound is that of muffled thunder carried by the vibration of the wings moving faster than the eye can follow.

The summer residents run into the dozens. Pine siskin sway back and forth on dandelion stalks, eating the seeds. The rufous hummingbird hovers over the brilliant fireweed. Violet-green swallows drop gracefully from the sky. Hundreds of the western evening grosbeak sweep by in one flock. The western tanager with his red head, yellow breast, and black wings is very much on parade. The western pileated woodpecker one sees at Goose Prairie is as big as a crow, some having a two-foot wingspread. I love to hear it hammering on an old Douglas fir. This magnificent bird gets so engrossed in tearing the wood apart that one can walk right up to him.

Old Scab, Buffalo, and Baldy—scarred summits that look down on Goose Prairie from the south—were welcome landmarks when, on a summer day, I trudged up the valley as a boy with a horse-shoe pack, headed for Bumping Lake and other ponds above and beyond it. Nowadays Double K, a comfortable rendezvous, looks across Goose Prairie to those peaks, whose moods change with the weather.

A day's journey west of Goose Prairie (and two thousand feet higher) is the Pacific Crest Trail, which runs the length of the State of Washington. It winds under and around huge volcanic cliffs and spires that suggest cathedrals still unfinished. Meadows line this trail and their eastern edges often drop sheer a thousand feet or more. This is a trail decorated by mountain hemlock and alpine fir. This is high country where the delicate pasqueflower is supreme and where the dwarf blueberry flourishes. Below this trail (on the east side) are many lakes.

Cougar Lake and its smaller companion lake at the base of House Mountains are favorite places where eastern brook trout thrive. The choice of all is Swamp Lake, one of the best we have for rainbow trout, running from twelve inches on up. Extensive stands of cedar mark the approach to Swamp Lake. This is the Alaska cedar, with thin, light gray bark and drooping boughs. It is the most fragrant of all our far-western trees; it thrives in damp soil; it reseeds well in the spongy land around Swamp Lake.

This lake country is right under the divide, where rain from the Pacific drips easily. On the average nearly four feet of rain come every year. Eight feet of snow are common. Twenty feet of snow are frequent. Forty feet occasionally arrive.

This is hallowed country where one walks softly. The cedar is so thick it shuts out direct sunlight; bracken are lush under foot. Deer, elk, bear, and coyote abound here. The traveler moves slowly and quietly if he desires to see them. Swamp Lake lies in a nest of marshlands. But a few mossy benches extend out from shore for the benefit of fishermen.

Behind Double K and to the north is American Ridge, which has a trail that rises sharply. It's a ridge dominated by alpine fir, a few white pine, some Douglas fir, and beautiful stands of ponderosa pine that lumbermen covet. They want to put a road up American Ridge and send the trees to market. That would be an act of desecration. This ridge would then be bald and ugly and soon eroded. It is now a serene place, commanding magnificent views. To the south are Goat Rocks and Mount Adams. To the north is Mount Baker and Glacier Peak of the northern Cascades. Mount St. Helens rises like a white cone against the western sky. Most startling of all is Mount Rainier, which rises from nearly sea level to 14,409 feet. Here on American Ridge it seems as if one can almost reach out and touch this giant of American peaks. Some of its twenty-six glaciers can be seen. The courses shaped by dozens of its waterfalls are visible. It is white and purple against fleecy clouds and so big and vast as to be equal in size to entire lesser ranges.

The trees on American Ridge rise in stately grandeur; and when the strong northwest winds blow the place is filled with the full music of the strings. Then is the time to lie flat and hear the bunch grass sing as it joins in the orchestration.

While I like American Ridge during all the seasons, I like it best in early Summer when the snow has not yet left the high ground. Then I have seen the bowl-like meadows carved from its sides completely carpeted with the dainty white and pink phlox. Jacob's ladder, with its blue, bell-shaped flowers, nods gracefully by the trail. Cinquefoil and lupine brighten harsh ravines with yellow and blue. The Oregon mallow, or wild hollyhock, grows here—a foot or so tall with miniature petals of pink. It has an air of domesticity about it even on the rough shoulders of American Ridge. If one goes early enough, he will also find acres of the creamy white trillium.

The flower that has left the deepest memory of American Ridge is the glacier lily. This golden beauty was found by Lewis and Clark and later by David Douglas. Its bulbs are eaten by bears. Some call it a dog's-tooth violet. By whatever name it goes, its beauty is transcendent. It is slightly darker than pure gold and dainty and delicate. Every time I see it on American Ridge I wonder how anything so exquisite can be made out of thin, harsh soil.

Mushrooms grow in splendor around Goose Prairie and along the trail south to Goat Rocks. We in America have never collected mushrooms as the Russians and eastern Europeans have done. Someone wrote that the mushrooms are the poor man's food and the rich man's delicacy. The folklore of many nations is rich in tales of the good and evil of mushrooms. There is an old saying in Russia that when mushrooms abound, war is in the offing. In history mushrooms have, in fact, been important food for displaced people wandering in the wilderness. We of the West have degraded the mushroom by giving it the repugnant name of toadstool. And the ones we have commercialized are second-and-third-class, compared with those from Goose Prairie. At Goose Prairie the morels, or sponge mushrooms, are the first to come in Summer. They have a head or cap that is pitted. The boletus come next in time. One species of boletus will cling to one type of tree, another to a different type. Some prefer aspen, some birch, some hemlock, some pine. This is a mushroom with an umbrella type of cap. One rather squat species with pale brownish cap and greenish yellow stalk is the famous *Boletus edulis*, known in Russia as the white mushroom because it is so delicious. A russet-red boletus is found under pine at Goose Prairie. A red-brown boletus is found on rotting hemlock logs. The boletus rank high in camp fare. The shaggy manes are also delicious. This is the *Coprinus comatus*—whose cap is oblong and bell-shaped. This shaggy-mane mushroom springs up after a rain and seems to love gravel, ashes, or the wet ground where cattails grow. Later come the puffballs which, if homogenous and white clear through, are delicious and nearly all safe to eat. The ones found in lodgepole pine and Englemann's spruce are especially sweet when sliced and fried in a batter of eggs and bread crumbs. We have at Goose Prairie huge coral mushrooms, growing at the base of conifers. They are usually buff colored and one of the choice products of our woods. Sometimes they run to fifty pounds, though the average size is much less. Here we find also the calves' brain mushroom that can be eaten with impunity once. But it is not recommended, for some people suffer if they eat a second mess. Much higher in the scales are the famed woods mushroom of the Pacific Northwest—the pure white clustered-icicle type that grows only on a fallen dead white fir. These will run as much as twenty pounds in weight.

When we make up a pack train and head for Goat Rocks from Goose Prairie, we are certain to have fresh, delicious mushrooms every night—the coral, the boletus, and the woods. Of the produce of the Cascades, they rank with the blueberries for flavor of distinction.

The trail out of Goose Prairie south to Goat Rocks rises sharply to a plateau studded with lakes, adorned with patches of fir, and decorated with flowers. Tumac Mountain—a cone-shaped peak of volcanic ash 6300 feet high that rises several hundred feet above the plateau—dominates the area and is the landmark for everyone. Blankenship Meadows lies immediately at the foot of Tumac. These meadows are lush and rich; and in June and early July every step into the soft sod sends upward a swarm of mosquitoes. When the meadows dry out a bit, when the squaw grass comes, they are more beautiful than any gardens I know.

They embrace about 400 acres. And when viewed from the air they are seen to be shaped roughly in the form of a cross. Alpine fir line the edges and appear in scattered clumps that break the sweep of the meadows. This fir that gives Blankenship Meadows distinction is so slim and pointed that Donald Culross Peattie once called it "an exclamation point." Those who stop to examine it closely will see that each tuft of needles seems to have been brushed upward into a graceful spire. Its branches are too short and stiff to bend even under the weight of great snows. It has been known to grow as high as 175 feet. But here in Blankenship Meadows it averages around sixty feet. It is a tree of such beauty and symmetry that it is one of the wonders of the ridges of the Cascades. It frames peaks, meadows, and the squaw grass to an artist's delight.

There is no place in the Cascades that squaw grass shows to greater advantage than in Blankenship Meadows. It is in many respects our most distinctive western flower. It is from two to four feet high, the base being a mass of broad, densely tufted leaves. A single stem shoots up from this base, having at its end cream-colored, plumelike spikes that are shaped into a round cone that ends with a nipple. Elk and deer like the blossoms. Bears dig up the tuberous roots in early Spring. The Indians boiled these roots to make soap. Squaws used its leaves in basketry. Hence the names sometimes given this member of the lily tribe—elk-grass, bear-grass, soap-grass, squaw-grass. Lewis and Clark collected the plant, calling it *Xerophyllum tenax,* which means "the dry leaf that holds fast." The name seemed appropriate because the squaws used the leaves to make vessels. They wove the leaves and cedar bark so closely that even without the use of gum or resin the vessels were watertight. This use, apart from the soap-producing quality, put the squaw grass in commerce up and down the Columbia River.

Blankenship Meadows are beautiful in a different way when Fall comes. The blueberry bushes then take over. They blaze scarlet in the sunshine. The Oregon grape brightens the woods with a deep port.

This plateau, dominated by Tumac Mountain, is part of the main ridge of the Cascades. Both east and west of the center are ponds and lakes. They are so numerous they seem without number. Many have fish. But, curiously, when I think of them my association is something other than their fish that have sustained me.

In memory, Apple Lake and Pear Lake always sparkle in sunshine as the wind whips up small waves. Brightly colored rainbow lie in wait there. But more poignant are recollections of the deep grass along the trail approaching them. Here the ground is moist and the Sierra rein orchis (sometimes called the white-flowered bog orchid) grows. It stands almost two feet tall and boasts a tapering spike of white, sweet-scented flowers. Nowhere else have I seen it so beautiful.

Twin Sisters Lakes lie a bit higher and the ground slopes away from them, making for drier soil. I was once on a fast canter near the lake, making time before it got too dark to fish. In spite of my haste I had to pull up, dismount, and get to my knees in a few moments of adoration. For I had come suddenly into an acre of bunchberry in bloom. It's related to the dogwood but much smaller, standing only a few inches high. Its four white flowers produce red berries in the Fall. This Summer they carpeted the ground, making as gay a display as dogwood ever did in eastern woods.

Frying Pan Lake, Snow Lake, and Jug Lake mean twelve- and fourteen-inch orange-bellied eastern brook trout. They also mean monkey flowers—both yellow and pink—that flourish in this wet, spongy land; the swamp laurel, whose saucer-shaped flowers are rose-purple; the more showy wake-robin with its three white, upright petals; and elk that bugle at me in the evening.

The eastern slopes of the Cascades are quite dry. Frying Pan, however, lies over the crest to the west. Moisture drips generously there; and with the summer storms comes an opaque fog that swallows men, horses, and tents. One must keep close to his companion or he'll lose him too. Once I traveled a complete circle in the fog, returning to Frying Pan Lake about two hours after I had left it.

The trail from Frying Pan Lake south to Goat Rocks swings from one side of the crest to the other, seldom traveling the crest itself. As one drops to the west side, climbs again, and swings over to the east slopes, Mount Rainier appears and disappears again and again. Alpine fir and Douglas fir dominate these ridges. Mountain hemlock is here too. It has grace and rare beauty. Its boughs curve gently downward; its slender leader nods graciously; its twigs reflect a soft, bluish green; its small, perfectly shaped cones cover the ground.

The plateau dominated by Tumac Mountain is high, parklike country. But once Cowlitz Pass is crossed, the trail drops rapidly for miles through a corridor of conifers. It crosses several benches where lakes are tucked away, and is lined with western laurel that blooms in late July and August. It is here I have found on rock ledges beside the trail the loveliest of all rose-pink penstemon. White Pass, once a primeval ravine where the mountain hemlock was thick and where the tamarack painted streaks of yellow in the Fall, is now laid with asphalt, where roaring cars break the solitude. A fine ski resort has been established there.

The trail—lined with high-bush blueberries—climbs steeply up Hogback Mountain. A small jewel of a lake, whose name is Slipper, lies to the left in a forested meadow. The steep climb is relieved by a few damp, open spaces hardly large enough to be called meadows but offering a fine reward. Here is the choice spring beauty, Siberian miner's lettuce, whose five pink petals are among the delicate creations of the universe.

Near the top of Hogback Mountain is a huge rock, running lateral to the ridge, named Thumb Rock. Once that is rounded, Goat Rocks stand in splendor to the south; and Shoe Lake—an exact imprint of a Paul Bunyan footprint nearly a mile long—is at one's feet. The open slopes leading down to the lake are rich in wild flowers. I have found there exquisite specimens of the orange-anthered saxifrage. One is under the glass top of my desk as I write. Pressed flat and dried, it has all the daintiness of a Japanese painting. In the Fall the low-bush blueberries are scarlet and the mountain ash is a rich cranberry. Then the effect is a a mass of red that fills the whole bowl. Summer or Fall, Shoe Lake sparkles with crystal-clear water. Its high banks and scattering of alpine fir make it a favorite campground. Now the Goat Rocks are less than a day away.

This, then, is Goose Prairie and the country it commands. Nursery of splendid trees. Garden of brilliant flowers. Abode of birds without number. Greenhouse for succulent mushrooms. Gateway to wild and high country, including the Goat Rocks. Home of friendly people.

Fall converts the Douglas maple, the willow, and the tamarack into gold and red flames. The leaves of the mountain ash are turning port, and its clusters of berries are bright red. Before long there will be spits of snow over Goose Prairie. An occasional lesser snow goose will drop in for a visit, and the Canadian geese—the great honkers for which Tom Fife named this meadow—will soar high overhead. This is the time of the year when the woods around this high prairie seem to hold their breath. Then I try to spend some hours with Jack Nelson. It is good for the soul to visit with him. He is an extra-good tonic for anyone who winters in Washington, D.C. Jack has such love of the wilderness that it permeates his whole being. I like to walk the woods with him when Fall sets the deciduous trees on fire with color.

Jack loves the trees at Goose Prairie as man loves pets. He had a word of admiration to say about the dozen or more species we saw, and he touched each one affectionately. He came to a Douglas fir that had recently been cut. It was four feet in diameter, and Jack had counted 550 rings.

"Think of it," he said. "This tree was here before Columbus was born." Jack went on to say that his study of the rings showed that back in the 1600s there was a period of thirty years when rainfall was scant at Goose Prairie.

"Five hundred years or more to make a tree and only a few minutes needed to destroy it," Jack observed. And then in a wistful way he added, "Wish some lumbermen could be taught that."

Back at Jack's log cabin we sat before an open fire of crackling tamarack while Kitty served tea. Jack chuckled as he told about a stranger who came up to him last Summer and asked, "You camped here?"

"What did you say?"

"I came running into the cabin to Kitty and asked her if she thought we were qualified as campers after only forty-eight years," said Jack. We all laughed; and then our conversation turned to birds. I asked Jack which was his favorite. He said they were all choice "bits of God." I pressed him for his preferences. He finally said, "For cheeriness, the water ouzel. How he can sing on a cold winter day! For wonderment, the winter wren. What great notes from such a tiny singer! For entertainment, the pileated woodpecker, hammering away on an old fir."

I asked him which bird he would choose for wisdom.

"The horned owl," he replied.

"Why?" I asked.

"It can beat the weatherman all hollow," Jack said.

"In what way?"

"When it hoots," he replied, "a storm is coming. When it laughs the weather will be mild."

To Jack and Kitty, Kay Kershaw, Elon Gilbert, and all who have come to know the area, Goose Prairie is the gateway to sanctuaries as precious as any that we Americans possess.

Each Fall, when I say farewell to my friends at Goose Prairie and head east, there are the same pleas.

"Don't let them commercialize our high basins."

"Don't let them cut any more trees."

"Don't let them build any more roads."

These are messages to the powers that be in Washington, D.C.

Kay Kershaw, whose heart is on the wind-blown ridges above Goose Prairie, says a special prayer for American Ridge. Greedy men have their eyes on it. Too few people have seen its glories.

Hence American Ridge enters the last half of the twentieth century with few friends to defend it. It needs help and protection from everyone who values glacier lilies and wind-blown pine not for dollars but for the mysteries and wonders which they reveal.

This back country faces another danger. Hunters are beginning to take short cuts. They now go in by helicopter, seeking to hunt elk and deer from the air. This is like chasing antelopes by jeep or swooping down on caribou or wolves from the air, shooting with machine guns. Man, with the power of the machine on his side, has an awful advantage. He then is not pitting his skills against animal life. He is using machines against flesh and blood; wildlife cannot long survive that.

"Like shooting big game at the zoo," was the way Kay put it.

CHAPTER VIII

GOAT ROCKS

THE Goat Rocks—midway between Mount Rainier and Mount Adams—are a true wilderness area. Here are the music of fast streams, the murmur of wind in alpine fir, goats on steep cliffs, elk in alpine meadows, and fleecy clouds casting shadows that race across massive walls of volcanic rock.

Surprise Lake, on the east, has a supply of fighting cutthroat trout. Above it is Warm Lake—a sapphire in a meadow bright with flowers. By midsummer the flowers on the slopes of Goat

Rocks run riot. This is lava rock, rich in phosphorus and potash. These chemicals plus the heat-absorbing qualities of the dark, volcanic rock produce a mass effect of wild flowers seen nowhere else.

There is no monotony in the architecture of Goat Rocks. Johnson Rock shows a dark wall several thousand feet high with snow on its shoulders. Old Snowy is a sharp crest, rising above perpetual snow fields. Ives Peak is a soft, sedate point. Tieton Peak is a half-finished pyramid. Devil's Horns is a ridge that looks like the head of the devil in a prone position. Gilbert Peak lifts broken volcanic fingers 8201 feet high.

I climbed these peaks many times, the first time as a boy. In my teens I camped many times on their shoulders. This was a favorite stamping ground for me and my boyhood companions. Bradley Emery, now with the Yakima papers, was one. He and I used the horseshoe pack, traveling the Goat Rocks country on foot. Douglas Corpron, now a physician in Yakima, also hiked these trails with me. Elon Gilbert, rancher and fruit broker, had horses, and he and I took many a pack train over these ridges and glaciers. Each peak of the Goat Rocks is therefore filled with nostalgic memories—Gilbert Peak especially, for it is the one we climbed most often. Once we carried to its top a copper capsule with a screw cap as holder for the register of those who make the climb. This we did in memory of another boyhood friend, Curtiss Gilbert, brother of Elon, who as Scout leader introduced many boys to the mountains.

One who comes to the Goat Rocks from Goose Prairie has his last camp at Shoe Lake. After Shoe Lake comes washboard country—up and down over low ridges and shallow valleys. If one travels it before the last snow has melted, there will be wonders to behold, for then the avalanche lily is at its best. The finest displays are probably on the lower slopes of Mount Rainier. But this washboard country is a close contender. This delicate white flower with an orange center thrives at the very edge of melting snowbanks. It makes one who sees it more reverent and humble. For it creates exquisite beauty out of extreme adversity.

This is country where great carpets of the bearberry, or kin-nikinnick, are found—the plant that mountain goats paw through the snow to reach. It has leathery leaves (which the Indians used for smoking, tanning, and dyeing) and pink, urn-shaped berries (which the Indians dried and used in cooking and that the grouse especially like). Our next camp after Shoe Lake is at McColl Basin, which lies at the very foot of Tieton Peak. The basin itself is one of the lush spots in the mountains. Water and grass are abundant, enough to hold horses all night. McColl Basin is also famous for its gorgeous tiger lilies, brilliant Indian hyacinth, and bright cinquefoil. And in the Fall there is no finer display of the blue gentian than McColl Basin puts on. McColl commands no great view. It's a good base of operations. Above it is Conrad Glacier, with caves to explore. Above it also are Tieton Peak and Old Snowy to climb. The stands of alpine fir on the fringes of this small meadow offer places for a protected camp. There is no sweeter music than that produced by the conifers when the great gales blow over Goat Rocks. And sunsets have a habit of setting the colored rocks of Tieton Peak aflame.

West Camp, which lies at the head of the Cowlitz River, is west of McColl Basin and on the ridge above it. At one place on this ridge are large deposits of obsidian rocks, broken into small pieces and lying loose on the surface of the ground. Once used by Indians for arrowheads, they now look like bright, shining flecks of newly made asphalt. Above West Camp is a narrow ridge leading to the top of Old Snowy. A climb of this ridge on an August day can be an experience that will enrich a lifetime. To the east and west are deep blue lakes tucked away in soft ravines. Rainier on the north, Adams on the south, St. Helens on the west are snow-white sentinels. This is a hogback ridge that drops off steeply in loose talus for several thousand feet on each side. The trail follows the narrow, pointed spine to the top and down the other side. This trail is only a few feet wide; the drop-off on each side is so great that some people get vertigo. It is indeed a bit like walking the cornice of the Empire State Building in New York City. My hours on this breath-taking ride are some of the most exhilarating of my life. I never have felt the thrill of wind as keenly as I have here. In August, while the draws and ravines leading to Goat Rocks are warm in sunshine, a blustering wind roars across Old Snowy. It comes with great gusto from the west. It is so strong that voices seem swept away almost before the words are uttered. While in meditation on this high ridge, I never have felt so remote from civilization, so far removed from the noise and clatter of cities, so distant from the roar of traffic. The ridge leading to Old Snowy is for me the choice place to untangle thoughts, to slough off tensions, to become a relaxed member of the family of Nature's children that inhabit the earth.

I remember John Muir's saying, "Most people are *on* the world, not in it . . . have no conscious sympathy or relationship to anything about them." On Old Snowy one becomes a part of something immense and universal.

We think of man as the favorite inhabitant of the earth. But on Old Snowy's heights I feel an affinity for the chipmunks that live among the prostrate juniper on this cold ridge. This is the Siberian juniper that seldom grows over a few inches high and spreads out to form large patches on barren ridges. Its decumbent branches form a thick mat and its needles, when broken, are strikingly pungent. I also feel an affinity for the mountain goats who frequent these ridges. These goats are deer-size and all white. The males have beards. The wool is soft and easily pulled out when it catches on rocks or brush. Evidence of their presence is in the little tufts of wool they leave behind—similar to the bits of themselves that judges leave behind when they decide cases. The goats were in these mountains when Lewis and Clark passed through the Columbia River Gorge. They thrive today. They never leave the heights for long. Even in Winter they stay high on the rocks, where steep slopes and strong winds keep the snow from their food supply. Summer and Winter their main forage is grass and sedges, with browse next. And among the browse the snowbrush, which covers many of the lower slopes of Goat Rocks in a tangle and fills the valleys with delicate perfume in June, is probably the favorite. In August and September they often go lower down for grass and browse. Yet not all of them leave. A billy sometimes appears around a rock so suddenly that I find myself six feet from the animal, yet unprepared for a photograph.

Cougars are probably the main predator, as they, too, are at home on the cliffs where goats seek refuge. Another predator is the eagle—both the bald and the golden—which I have seen diving on kids on the ledges of Goat Rocks. How many kids become victims of these attacks is not known. Yet it is true, I think, that one formidable enemy comes down from the skies. The eagles and the cougars, however, must both take second place. For now that the hunting season has been opened for goats, man has become the chief predator of all.

The botanical display on the slopes below Old Snowy has infinite beauty. The species in bloom at one time run into the dozens. Acres upon acres of Indian paintbrush are at one's feet. Infinite varieties of flowers are blended into patterns of blue, yellow, purple, and pink. Most daring of all are the vast blue carpets of lupine and of white and lavender phlox. These are the dwarf species that lie like lavender or white scatter rugs on the cold shoulders of the ridge. The earth is harsh and skimpy; the flowers delicate and dainty. I pay like tribute to the dwarf lupine. It manufactures humus out of coarse sand on these barren slopes by drawing nitrogen from the air and transmitting it to the soil. Even on the cold hogback ridge wild flowers have taken hold. The sturdy saxifrage makes a bold stand there. And nowhere else have I seen larkspur so rich in purple. The silky phacelia shows blue against the dark rocks; the tiny Pacific stonecrop and the fern-leaf fleabane brighten the ridge with touches of yellow. The heavy-leaved oar-leaf eriogonum shows pink. There is white rock cress on this wind-blown ridge and yellow willowweed, both dwarf and miniature. The sturdy western yarrow is present. Sandwort—a delicate-looking plant with white flowers that is found up to 12,000 feet or more in our western mountains—thrives on Old Snowy. So does a dwarf collomia with grayish-green leaves and orange flowers. On this harsh ridge that looks sterile at first glance plants indeed thrive.

Alpine fir straggles up the lower reaches of the ridge. Higher up with the juniper is the alpine whitebark pine that adds grandeur to these bleak areas. On Old Snowy this whitebark pine is only knee-high. Yet the branches are so well nourished that they can be tied into knots like a rope.

Packwood Glacier on the west and Meade and Conrad Glaciers on the east are relics of the ice age, when long tongues of ice scoured the sides of the Cascades and built moraines in the lower reaches. Sentimentally I am greatly drawn to Meade Glacier.

Warm Lake, hardly larger than a pond, lies close to its edge. Its water becomes warm by afternoon on a July or August day; its white sandy beach is always an invitation. Doug Corpron and I often used it as our swimming hole. It is fringed by the dwarf whitebark pine and the Alaska cedar. This cedar, the most sorrowful of all the conifers because of its drooping foliage, grows a hundred feet high in the western Cascades. At Warm Lake it is dwarfed and puny.

The slopes beneath Meade Glacier are filled with meadows rich in alpine bunch grass. In the Summer they are ablaze with flowers so thickly matted they produce the effect of a rich Chinese or Persian rug. Once Doug Corpron and I marked a spot about three feet square and counted thirty species of flowers in bloom there. Pink, yellow, blue, red, white, cerise, purple, port, cinnamon were blended into patterns beautiful beyond words. The violets, buttercups, and saxifrage are the most delicate I know. Indian hyacinth is lush here. Indian paintbrush is everywhere. Here are the bottle gentian, whose blue petals are never completely open. A bee can enter the flower only by pressing at the apex. If it went completely in, there would be no way out. The bees of the Goat Rocks know this. For they only half enter the bottle gentian, holding the door open with their rear legs. The choice of all is the red and white heather which thrives in these acid soils. The waxy flowers are bell-shaped. They grow so thick and are so closely matted they give a light blush to hundreds of acres.

The ptarmigan love the blossoms. The white-tailed ptarmigan flourishes on the Goat Rocks. When Winter comes, the bird turns white; its claws grow long and pointed for walking over icy slopes; and the openings of its nose at the base of the bill are set with dense, close feathers to keep out the frost and fine snow. The freezing blasts of air, the bright light, the dwarfed and wind-blown vegetation, the extensive snow and ice fields of the Goat Rocks provide the arctic conditions under which these birds thrive. In Summer their color changes. Their wings, tail, and belly stay white, while their upper parts become mottled with brown and black. This lovely creature is with us the year around, moving off the high slopes in Winter but never leaving the area. Beneath Gilbert Peak it is so well camouflaged in Summer that I have almost stepped on one. They have gentle habits. Even when startled they do not depart with a roar but leave politely and discreetly.

There are not many birds at this elevation. Horned larks are far out over Meade Glacier. Here, too, are the pipits, which seem to walk, rather than hop, and dip up and down in flight. An ancient legend has followed the pipits to the Cascades. It is said that they followed Mary and Joseph with the infant Jesus when fleeing Egypt, and helped the party escape those in pursuit by using their long tails to brush out of the sand the tracks of the donkey. On the edges of the forests of alpine fir the varied thrush, with orange breast marked by a black band, nests. On the ridge above the glacier are hummingbirds. High on the glacier itself are the black rosy finch and the Oregon junco. These are sometimes called the "refrigerator birds," for they feed on insects that have been caught in the ice and snow fields—and on the snowworms that inhabit the glaciers. On Meade Glacier the insects are mosquitoes (which were probably products of wet alpine meadows) and small flies that may have come in under their own power.

On the Goat Rocks I have seen hordes of grasshoppers arrive out of the void and descend on the high meadows. I have also seen a host of white butterflies appear from nowhere to swarm over a thick bed of dwarf phlox. Butterflies migrate. Some move from Mexico as far north as the St. Lawrence, a distance of 3000 miles. Hundreds of millions have made this migration. Another species, the monarch, settles on trees in southern California for semihibernation and moves north in the Spring some 1500 miles. The mates travel together, laying their eggs on the milkweed as it first appears above the ground, thus repopulating the earth.

Dr. Charles H. Abbott has studied the migrations of the painted-lady butterfly from California and has discovered that these migrations are the result of overpopulation. Dr. C. B. Williams has found that about 300 species of butterflies migrate; and he concludes that many of those migrations come when the population reaches outbreak proportions. When the population burgeons, parasites, including wasps and flies, move in on the larvae and the balance is restored.

These migrations of butterflies are a world-wide phenomenon. Though they usually fly about ten feet from the ground, they go up several thousand feet to get advantage of any tail wind. If they meet an obstacle in their flight they go over it rather than around it. Where my white-winged friends on the Goat Rocks hibernated, where they were going, I never knew.

I learned from my Goat Rocks experiences that many other insects migrate—flying thrips, aphids, crickets, beetles, flies. Some migrations may be short dispersal flights. Others may be hundreds of miles long. Some go under their own wing power. Some, who have weak power for flight, spin waxy filaments and silken threads that serve as balloons, increase their buoyancy, and carry them long distances. Some aphids apparently move that way. Others are picked up by the wind and carried long distances. Whence came the tiny flies refrigerated by Meade Glacier, I do not know. Perhaps they flew there on a migration that played a part in their manifest destiny. Perhaps they were blown there. Perhaps something happened to tip the balance of nature and give them a head start over other insects. They may have been the debris of some mass outbreak. Many insects migrate in search of food. Perhaps the derelicts in the ice of Meade Glacier were hungry, like the locust that move north over Persia.

In any event the Oregon juncos and the black rosy finches were the beneficiaries. And they eat in style from the supply of fresh frozen food that Meade Glacier furnishes.

While Goose Prairie is my favorite starting point for a trek to the Goat Rocks, Mount Adams on the south is next. This approach has some advantages, for the southern massif of the Goat Rocks is in sight for miles on end. The black peaks, draped with snow and glaciers, have a great magnetism. When the trail drops and sight of them is temporarily lost, I always feel an eagerness to reach the next height where I can see them again. As they once more come into view, a strange excitement possesses me. It is the excitement I found among monks in the Himalaya who were on a pilgrimage and finally saw their holy place in the distance. The Goat Rocks seem holy to me—of this earth and yet apart from it. They are sanctuaries built on such a vast scale that he who approaches them from the south is certain to feel humble and reverent.

This trail from the south crosses lush country where mountain ash—never more than a dozen feet high—has rich splendor. Yet if its creamy bloom has passed, there is the reward of the lovely Cascade azalea that displays showy white blossoms. This is also the country of the low-bush blueberry that matures in early August. Wild strawberries flourish here. Stately mountain hemlock and noble red fir are on display. Tiger lilies and columbine are in abundance. Some talus slopes are bright with larkspur. This south side of the Goat Rocks carries patches of snow most of the year. The higher one climbs and the closer one gets to these pinnacles the richer the bunch grass. The valley below Cispus Pass (6473 feet) is a bowl about a mile wide and several thousand feet deep. Its sides are rich in grass, and if the timing is right, this entire bowl will be filled with squaw grass in bloom. The trail keeps right under the rim of this vast bowl for over a mile. There is such depth, such sweep to these slopes under Cispus Pass that I always feel I am facing infinity. Yet it is not a void I see. For the creamy white of the squaw grass and the bright blue of the lupine make this the most glorious amphitheater I have seen any-where in the world.

There are bright-blue alpine speedwell along the trail and herds of elk in the stands of alpine fir that mark these slopes. The slate-colored cowbird follows every animal that moves, eating the insects that are stirred up from the grass. A hummingbird streaks across the ridge. And as long as one stays high, there is always Adams to the south, St. Helens to the west, and the Goat Rocks to the north to lift the heart.

One fine reward of this approach to Goat Rocks is a night or two at Corral Lake that lies a mile or so to the south of Cispus Pass. Lava buttes command the lake. Deer and elk frequent it. This is a place of remoteness, seldom visited. One feels he is now in one of the sacred precincts of the hills.

At Corral Lake I sat by the fire, studying maps of the Cascades. I soon reached a conclusion that holds good throughout most of America. Apart from Alaska, there are few places left where one can get more than ten miles from any road. This country between Adams on the south and Rainier on the north was largely roadless when I first knew it. If we kept to the high country, we could hike for weeks without reaching a road of any kind. Now there are jeep roads and main highways over which the tourists throng. Few, if any, ever come on foot. Recreation is where the automobile can go.

The car is our leash that keeps us confined to a small radius. We seldom get out of sight of it. The pull of the wilderness is not strong enough to lead us on and on for hours, or even days, to search out the secrets of nature. The car is the true magnet. It determines where we go and what we do.

This night at Corral Lake I also thought of Ram Rahul, an Indian, who, after being my guide and interpreter when I crossed the Himalaya, came to this country to do graduate work at Harvard. He had been there only a month when he spent a weekend with me in Washington, D.C.

"Tell me, what do you think of America?" I asked.

He was plainly embarrassed. It took persuasion to make him talk. Finally this sensitive soul, who had hiked and ridden muleback with me for about 250 miles over high and rough terrain, replied, "I think America is too soft for the troubled days ahead."

"Why?"

"At Harvard," he finally said, "the farthest classroom is six blocks from my dormitory. I am the only one who walks. The rest go by car."

The network of roads over the Cascades were proving my Indian friend's observation. America is on the move. But it is the car, not man, that does the work. Only a few leave civilization to rejoin nature and become once more an elemental part of the wilderness. The thrill of tramping alone and unafraid through a wildness of lakes, creeks, alpine meadows, and glaciers is not known to many. A civilization can be built around the machine. But it is doubtful if a meaningful life can be produced by it.

When man worships at the feet of avalanche lilies or discovers the delicacy of the pasqueflower, or finds the faint perfume of the phlox on rocky ridges, he will come to know that the real glories are in God's creations. When he feels the wind blowing through him on a high peak or sleeps under closely matted white-bark pine in an exposed basin, he is apt to find his relation to the universe.

CHAPTER IX

GLACIER PEAK

I SAT on a knife-edged ridge in the northern Cascades, lost in thought. At my back the canyon dropped sheer for two thousand feet. The south slope at my feet made up into a deep, grassy bowl. Coming up, I had discovered that this bowl was dotted with painted cups—some yellow, some red. I had also found on these south slopes an amazing variety of lousewort. The one that caught my fancy was the elephants' heads. It has a purplish stem with a crowded spike of many flowers, shaped like little elephant heads, slightly fragrant, and deep pink in color. There were tiger lilies in abundance. Heather—some white, some lavender—made gay streaks. And the bees were busy in it. The pasqueflower—now in seed—showed its dainty plumes. A wide variety of sedges covered this bowl, and oval-leafed bilberry bushes—some in fruit that would soon be ripe—made up a large portion of the ground cover. In some hollows currant bushes grew luxuriantly; and this August their branches were heavy with deep-red fruit. Mountain ash was brilliant with its red berries.

There was, to my surprise, very little bunch grass here. The sides of this bowl had innumerable trails made by the deer and mountain goats. Sheep had once been in here, and they did their usual damage. This bowl at my feet already showed signs of washing. This is indeed fragile land, whose thin topsoil clings precariously to the sharp pitches of the canyons.

A bright buttercup, hardly an inch high, greeted me as I reached the tip. And a patch of grayish-green lupine, whose flowers were so tiny they almost went unnoticed, offered me a resting place.

This ridge was no more than 7000 feet high. Yet it was above tree line. The pines, the hemlock, the cedars were far below me. Only a few alpine fir with small purple cones that brightened their crowns were in this life zone; and I had left the last clump of them a few hundred feet down.

Glacier Peak (10,436 feet) higher than all Washington mountains except for Rainier, Adams, and Baker, dominated the southern skyline. It was draped with glaciers. Everywhere I looked there were peaks showing glaciers. These mountains lie so close to the Pacific that they are beneficiaries of most of its moisture. Each year's snowfall is deep, and packs down into permanent snow fields and gradually builds into the blue ice of living glaciers that hang permanently on the precipitous shoulders of these peaks.

The glacier that dug out the chasm where Lake Chelan lies was seventy-five miles long. One who travels to the head of Stehekin Valley can see several living fragments of it. Most of the glaciers in the northern Cascades are now small; and some send tons of debris into their canyons on warm days. Some are fast receding. Others are great tumbles of *séracs* and crevasses. Some ice fields make up into a radial glacier system that was characteristic of the ice age. And some of these living glaciers are extensive, Honeycomb on Glacier Peak extending more than three miles.

Some of the northern Cascades are lava. Glacier Peak is indeed a volcanic cone. Pumice—so light it will float in water—is found here. Near Red Pass at the headwaters of the Whitechuck River, southwest of Glacier Peak, is the site of an old blowhole where a hill of pumice was ejected and piled in the fashion of a mound of tailings at the entrance of a drift. Pumice also lies at great depth in the river valleys of the Chiwawa and Entiat. Granite joined basalt when the earth's surface folded and buckled. These upturned slabs formed great massifs, commanding steep canyons. Some walls are as highly polished as those in Yosemite. There are shales, limestone, and sandstone here too. And the grays of granite often shade into pinks and reds.

These peaks—which someday will be ranked with our greatest ones—are as yet little known. Glacier Peak is not visible from any major highway. Foothills hide the alpine area. The peaks are locked into a remote area that is a true recluse. This inner realm is remote and exquisite. Man did not plan it that way. The Glacier Peak area is a wilderness by sheer accident. Civilization so far has passed it by. A miner's helicopter is sometimes seen. High overhead a passenger plane makes a fleeting passage. But there are not many noises apart from those made by wind and water.

The view from any ridge in this range shows more snow and ice than any of our mountains south of Alaska. This is also a land that bursts with cascades of cold, clear water. Every ravine, every canyon has crystal-clear streams. High meadows spout ice-cold creeks. All of the water is safe to drink. It is pure distillation from a true wilderness.

On this lonely ridge I was not more than two days' hike from road's end. Yet it seemed I had left civilization far, far behind. I was so remote from cities and factories and farms that it seemed I was on another planet. Will the next generation ever have the chance to experience the same feeling of serenity and composure that comes when man faces the wilderness alone? This was my soliloquy as Cragg Gilbert, following a different route, joined me. I put the question to him and we talked a half hour or more about it.

If the population of this nation doubles by the end of this century (as it will if present trends continue), all the country along the coast from the Canadian border to Eugene, Oregon, will be one continuous urban and suburban area. The Pacific Northwest will be as saturated with population as Los Angeles is today. The sea will be one escape from civilization; the mountains another. The Glacier Peak area, if left roadless and intact, will offer perpetual physical and spiritual therapy. For its rugged nature—its steep canyons, forbidding glaciers, and knife-edged ridges—will be a magnet to those who have daring and fortitude.

"There should be some training grounds for them," Cragg added.

I mentioned John Muir's comparison of wild mountain sheep and domestic sheep. He found the latter quite dull, the former exciting. Nature builds strength and character competitively. Domesticated animals, like men and women of cities, get lazy habits. They become dependent on others, losing the drive and initiative that marked the species in the beginning. This loss of character can be disastrous to a race of men who, apartment-born, never experience the challenge that nature demands of all her children. This race of apartment-born people is of the earth, yet not a vital part of it. It is coddled and protected, utterly dependent on machines for its existence. It does not know how to pit human ingenuity against the universe; it therefore has no key to survival against disaster.

Men need testing grounds to develop these capacities. They cannot flower at Coney Island or at the ball park. Men need to know the elemental challenges that sea and mountains present. They need to know what it is to be alive and to survive when great storms come. They need to unlock the secrets of streams, lakes, and canyons and to find how these treasures are veritable storehouses of inspiration. They must experience the sense of mastery of adversity. They must find a peak or a ridge that they reach under their own power alone.

Cragg and I were disturbed. Before striking into the heart of the northern Cascades we had scouted its fringes. Roads were threatening at most points of the compass. On the west a road has already crept within a mile or so of Cascade Pass. Another presses into Bridge Creek from the east. Some, coming in from the south, are pointed like daggers at the heart of this remote area.

This is not the only threat. Forest Service plans call for the logging of some of the deep, narrow valleys that lie at the foot of Glacier Peak. Suiattle is one; Agnes is another. These are low valleys as far western country goes. We had come in by Lake

Chelan (1100 feet), meeting Ray Courtney at Stehekin and packing in from there. We traveled the South Fork of Agnes Creek,
reaching Suiattle Pass (5983 feet) in two days. At the start there
were song sparrows and rattlesnakes, and with them poplar, alder,
willow, and ponderosa pine. Raspberries and blackberries were
thick. There was the fragrant snowbrush in these lower reaches,
and much ocean spray. These—including the song sparrows and
snakes—were soon left behind. White firs and red firs appeared,
and in their shade I saw the bright-leaved Oregon grape, a host
of the delicate twinflower, and masses of meadow foam. The
forest floor is thick with kinnikinnick. Vine maple flourishes
here. The snowberry—the bush that Lewis and Clark brought
back from their expedition and that Jefferson sent to Paris as a
decorative plant—is abundant. Its red flowers had gone when we
traveled Agnes Creek and its white pulpy fruit was well formed.
This fruit has two seeds greatly loved by chipmunks. They re-
move the seeds quite deftly, leaving only the pulp. They were
beginning their snowberry harvest as we passed.

Higher up the canyon came the western hemlock, the Alaska
cedar, and the red cedar. They flourish at a three-thousand-foot
altitude, growing to immense size. They are the plums in the
Agnes Creek pudding that the lumbermen want. And the Forest
Service seems bent on letting them have what they want.

This hemlock-cedar forest is an inspiring sight. The shade is
so thick that no grass grows. The tall, delicious blueberry grows
lush. Somewhat below it stands the slim Solomon plume with
strikingly translucent leaves. Lower still is the baldhip rose.
There's a fourth bush that is more associated with the Pacific
coast line than the Cascades. It is the devil's club, whose stalks
bristle with spines but whose young leaves deer and horses adore.

These four, in the main, make up the understory of the hemlock-cedar forest.

Agnes Creek Canyon is for the most part a narrow, V-shaped valley. The waters of the creek are clear and cold. They form one cascade after another, and below each is a deep pool where rainbow trout, pointed upstream, watch for morsels that are washed down.

The canyon is so narrow for much of the way that there is hardly room for more than the trail and the creek. There are not many places that offer the room necessary for tents and campfires. We stopped at one, and my small Himalayan tent had to crowd close to the trail. The truth is that a road up Agnes Creek—which would be built if this canyon were lumbered—would occupy most of the space. A road would not serve the purposes of recreation for those who come by car. The valley has few broad reaches where camp sites could be erected for the motorist. Agnes Creek, with its sharp canyon walls and its skimpy ground cover, would wash terribly. Agnes Creek—now as clear and pure as wildness can make any water—would run mud and silt. Lumber interests would be served; the man who built the road would make a fortune—but the harsh gully that would be left would stand for decades as a monument to the folly of an age that has tried to convert man into a statistic. That act of desecration would prove that the powers that be downgrade values that cannot be converted into dollar signs. What is true of Agnes Creek is in large measure true of Suiattle Creek, also doomed to being raped by saw and ax.

The Glacier Peak area is so little known it has few friends. Those bent on exploiting it, therefore, have a great advantage. They hope to perfect their plans before the public is aware of the great treasure that is here. The Forest Service is under the pressure of these powerful interests to do their bidding. The men in government who will decide the fate of this invaluable bit of wilderness have themselves not seen it. Even the local Forest Service men have probed very, very few canyons and high meadows. Who then will defend the Glacier Peak area?

These were the things Cragg and I discussed on a high ridge before we climbed Plummer Peak (7870 feet). Back in camp at Image Lake, we took up where we had left off. Bill Obertauffer, who had brought a group of Mazamas into Image Lake, joined us as the sun was setting. We stood on a knoll fringed by alpine fir, watching the sun turn the ice of Glacier Peak purple and then red. Suiattle River lay below us. The dark green of conifers filled this rich valley. Instead of deep forests where boys and girls would walk quietly and reverently as they approached the sanctuaries of Glacier Peak, there might soon be ugly stumps. Image Lake—whose value in terms of sheer beauty and inspiration is incalculable—was also threatened. For Miner's Ridge, where it lies, is to be left out of the proposed wilderness area. The reason? Mining interests want to chew it up in search of copper.

I mentioned that scientists had discovered that one ton of granite contains about four grams of uranium and twelve grams of thorium. Nuclear management could get out of these properties energy equivalent to that released on the burning of fifty tons of coal. "Now we can find new uses for our granite mountains," I sarcastically added.

"Think of putting any of these peaks or ridges through a rock crusher," Bill said. "How sacrilegious can we get?"

The exposure of Miner's Ridge to spoliation by mining interests seemed unthinkable to those of us who knew it and had come to love it. The gutting of Suiattle Valley, which lies at the feet of Glacier Peak, seemed equally profane. Harsh gullies and ugly wasteland would take the place of deep, dark forests that now are the haunts of deer, cougar, bobcat, wolverine, and bear. Glacier Peak would tower over a wasteland where gullies had been washed clear of topsoil.

This is not a speculative matter. Clear-cutting in the Far West produces deep scars on slopes. A canyon of trees restful to the eyes is invariably supplanted by a canyon of rocks and debris. A harvest of pine in Florida or Georgia means a new crop a few decades hence. But the harvest of the timber in the canyons of our western mountains often produces torrential runoffs of water that turn a fertile place into a sterile wasteland. The Cascades are cruelly scarred by these operations. Thousands of years will pass before vegetation can produce the humus necessary for a new forest.

Cragg, Bill, and I talked of these things. The emphasis which these two sturdy mountaineers gave to the spiritual values of the wilderness reminded me of a meeting I had attended where federal fieldmen had discussed protests by citizens of plans for spraying sagebrush land. They roared with laughter when it was reported that a little old lady opposed the plan because the wild flowers would be destroyed.

Yet was not her right to search out a painted cup or a tiger lily as inalienable as the right of stockmen to search out grass or of a lumberman to claim a tree? The aesthetic values of the wilderness are as much our inheritance as the veins of copper and coal in our hills and the forests in our mountains.

This idea came back to me again and again as I traveled the northern Cascades. Never have I seen such a wealth of views. Every ridge opens visions that halt one in his steps and produce sheer wonder and amazement. "This is country where one looks either up or down," Cragg had said. There are peaks too numerous to count. Each one is a study in elegance and distinction. Some are spires; some are rounded domes. Some drop sheer; others have tiny ledges dotted with lichens and sprinkled with purple penstemon. There are ridges so narrow two people cannot walk abreast. There are great black fortresses sprinkled with snow. Others show miles of serrated skyline, whose sharp points cut the sky like the teeth of a saw. One does, indeed, look down into an abyss at his feet or up to an icy pinnacle touching the sky. Water roars off some cliffs and forms into vapor as it falls. Glaciers have a dazzling splendor in brilliant sunshine. Narrow saddles beckon one on and on; and when he reaches a pass he looks down into another canyon of mystery. The canyons are deep and narrow, some guarded by talus slopes, others deeply wooded. The ideal way to travel is cross-country—over one ridge, down a few thousand feet to the bottom, and up the next ridge. This is travel for men with back packs. Many canyon walls are too steep for horses. This is country for unhurried travel. The pitches are too steep for those on the run. The wonders are too startling for those in a hurry. One who mounts a ridge needs to sit there for some hours, attentive and relaxed. Then the beauties of this creation are absorbed and become a part of him. They set up a rhythm that restores all cells to a healthy harmony. There are some secrets of Glacier Peak that require patience to discover.

The Oregon wintergreen shows greenish white along the trails. Tiny white orchids (*Habenaria*) grow alternately on a stem hardly six inches high. The beautiful queencup bead-lily—whose white flower stands guarded by two large pointed leaves— brightens shaded areas. Some flowers, like the Sitka valerian, are bold and showy, making their presence known. So is the Cascade azalea, whose creamy white flowers streak across a hillside.

Shooting stars are gay in open meadows. But the bright trillium is almost hidden in the litter of the forest floor. The buttercups I have mentioned are also more retiring. The Mount Rainier cinquefoil, with tiny yellow flower heads, hides behind granite rocks. The yellow elkslip marsh marigold is a treasure found in recesses seldom visited because they are tucked away under high cliffs. The purplish Cusick speedwell and the bright blue alpine speedwell are often solitary guardians of wind-blown ridges. When one reaches the snow fields he is almost certain to find in August glacial lilies showing dark gold. Here, too, are beds of phlox more fragrant than the mantles formed by the white and lavender heather. And, where the talus leaves sharp ridges to form hillsides that the frost moves ever downward, a small, sturdy saxifrage—*Saxifraga pectimata*—is a reward for one with patience.

Alpine basins also offer rich rewards. There are yellow monkey flowers where cool water drips over bright green moss. Spring beauties are everywhere in these high, damp places. The delicate yellow-flowered lanceleaf is the daintiest of these. The squat yellow groundsel—*Senecio subnudus*—is almost concealed by bunch grass. And high on some slopes or ridges is a tree unique to the Pacific Northwest. It is the alpine larch, found only in these northern Cascades. It is a tree that has a stunted appearance. Yet its red-brown bark and smooth gray branches give it a dignified appearance, though it is scraggly. When Fall comes, the leaves turn bright gold and make the northern Cascades gay. Then they drop, and for eight or nine months the larch stands naked. Yet year round it has character in keeping with the rigorous regime of these ridges where bitter winds blow.

Mountain goats are often not conspicuous. But they, too, offer surprises. Plummer Peak at the top is hardly wide enough for one man. Yet when Ray Courtney climbed it, he found a billy in firm possession.

There are ruffed grouse lower down, and closer to the top are blue grouse who go out with a roar, flying low with a great sweeping movement. Here, too, are ptarmigan so well camouflaged that one may almost step on the bird before its presence is known.

Mule deer bed down in stands of alpine fir during the bright hours. A golden eagle, king of this vast domain, catches the high currents of air and soars the canyons. Chipmunks and golden-mantled ground squirrels move nervously under these wings that bring death down from the skies. For when the golden eagle strikes, he comes with the speed of lightning, stunning his prey with a violent blow of his elbow. Then he turns in flight and retrieves his feast.

One of the choice rewards of the northern Cascades is the hoary marmot. It's about twenty inches long. Its head is short and broad; its body thickset. Its ears are short; its eyes small. The face is black; the back is gray; the rump is black streaked with gray; the tail is brown. It has runways under the rocks that lead to feeding grounds. It is a vegetarian, collecting food in the field and bringing it back to the den, where it is eaten. Its enemies are the golden eagle, the coyote, and, to a lesser extent, the bear. It hibernates from late Fall to early Summer.

I have visited with these marmots for hours on end. They have a long, clear whistle. Its single note is repeated over and again; and one who answers excites the animal's curiosity. I have exchanged whistles with these charming creatures until I was within six feet of them. Only then was the danger signal sounded, and they disappeared in a rockslide as if swallowed up.

The high lakes are jewels set in lush meadows. Those, like Lyman, that are fed by streams running off glaciers have a turquoise-green tinge caused by glacial silt. Most of them are deep, dark blue in color. They have rainbow, eastern brook, and cutthroat trout. Some, like Trapper and Canyon, are off the beaten trails and offer rich rewards to one who invests the energy to get there. Once I visited Canyon Creek Lake on foot. It lies under Totem Pass, which this season was heavy with snow. I dallied as I went, stopping every half mile or so to soak up some of the grandeur of this wilderness. After a stiff climb through a forest of hemlock and fir, I came to an unnamed meadow that is a paradise on earth. It is perhaps a mile short of Canyon Creek Lake and somewhat lower. It lies on a small shelf protruding from the canyon wall. It drops off sharply on its south side into the canyon I had climbed. Some miles across intervening canyons stands Glacier Peak in all its glory. Clumps of mountain hemlock and white fir fringe this meadow. A host of grasshoppers greeted me. Then came a lone robin. Juncos en route to some snow field higher up where refrigerated insects are to be found stopped momentarily and then went their way. I stopped at a small creek that murmured as it crossed this meadow, and put my face in it. Then I stood for some moments absorbing the scene. Mountain goats had left some scat near the creek. But there was no other sign that this meadow had been used. There were perhaps twenty acres of thick and lush grass. I scouted the outer edges, looking for ashes of old campfires. But apparently no one had stopped here. This was a pristine meadow, revealing all the glory that God had bestowed on it. It was a high balcony seat overlooking the universe. This nameless wonder is not the only meadow that is as fresh and beautiful as wildness itself. There are countless others in the northern Cascades. Some never touched by man. Some never seen by human eyes. They are tucked away on high shelves or in remote basins for those yet unborn to discover. Their wonder, their glory, their excitment are one of our priceless assets—worth more than timber prices or market quotations for copper stocks will ever reveal. These deep, dark canyons, these bright, lush alpine meadows are the finest bequests we can leave to those who follow. If the valleys and ridges of this Glacier Peak area are sealed from commercial projects, we will have forever in America high country of enchantment. Those who search them out will learn that an emptiness in life comes with the destruction of wilderness; that a fullness of life follows when one comes on intimate terms with woods and peaks and meadows. Then a person learns that he was born not to destroy the chain of life of which he is a part but to nourish it; that he owes respect not only to his elders but to the snow buttercup at his feet and the hoary-mantled marmot, whistling to him from a rockslide. This lovely, nameless meadow has such a hold on me that I revisit it in memory every day of my life.

Our last night in the northern Cascades was spent at Lyman Lake. A biting wind drove the temperature down to freezing. Squalls sent stinging sleet across the range. A deep fog moved in from the west and played around Bonanza Peak (9511 feet). Downdrafts sucked the black fog earthward; and then it was swirled upward again in a frenzied movement. New black fog kept pouring in from the west. The night promised to be a bitter one.

There are two lakes at Lyman, and the upper one lies under Lyman glacier, which occupies a huge cirque on the north slopes of Chiwawa Mountain. I climbed up to it and found, on the edge of the basin where the upper lake lies, a thick stand of alpine fir. Deer went out ahead of me; and I discovered that this stand of dwarf fir was a place where they bedded down. I followed their example and entered the dense stand, sitting down and facing Bonanza Peak. This was excellent protection from the cold wind —a place where a man could survive the night. But my presence alarmed a group of several dozen white-crowned sparrows. They swooped above me, returning several times to protest my visit. The sun came out briefly, caught the moisture in the wet fog that was swirling over the mountain, and formed a radiant rainbow. It disappeared as quickly as it came; a marten crossed the trail below me; and darkness had descended by the time I could return to camp.

The Engelmann's spruce sang a boisterous song all night. The storm was gone by sunup, but the chill lingered on. Not until we neared Holden, where the yellow pine flourishes and the porcupine multiply, were our backs warm again. This is trail's end, where I said farewell to Ray Courtney. This tall, lean mountain man of few words knows the northern Cascades better than any living person. He has seen it through all the seasons and has slept in most of its basins. Each peak is a familiar friend. He knows the life that is nourished by this range and the wonders of it all. He speaks of Glacier Peak with reverence, and he respects every canyon and every slope. He has drawn on the resources of these mountains for his sustenance, taking fish, grouse, goat, and deer for meat and gathering berries for his table. But he never took more than he needed, and he always fought hard in the councils at Stehekin to keep greed out of the northern Cascades. He knows the spiritual values represented here, and he is alarmed at the plans which timber and mining interests have for it.

When he shook my hand and said good-by, he added:

"Don't let them destroy these mountains."

This parting message came through with deep emotion, for

Ray believes that anyone who knows the Glacier Peak country as he and Cragg and I know it cannot help but love it. And no one in his right mind destroys what he loves.

Back in Washington, D.C., I read the hearings on the Forest Service's proposal to exclude from this wilderness area the valleys below Glacier Peak and open them to lumber operations. I learned that most of the witnesses opposed the Forest Service plan and that those who backed it expressed values of wilderness solely in terms of dollars. The testimony of one business analyst stated the matter without equivocation:

> Let us calculate just what happens to the economy of our State when we remove from our timber wealth one million board feet of timber by locking it up in roadless wilderness:

Loss of Direct Employment	13.3 persons
Loss of Payroll	$ 58,750
Loss of Direct Support	45 persons
Loss of Forest Products	$180,000
Loss of Stumpage Values	$ 20,000
Loss to County	$ 5,000
Loss of Roads and Trail Fund	$ 2,000
Loss to United States Treasury	$ 13,000

Sawmills are important in our economy. Yet sawmills should not devour all our green valleys. Of the 24 million acres of forest lands in the State of Washington, over 80 per cent are already being commercially used. What remains untouched are mostly small islands—tiny, compared with the whole, and not critical to the economy. Yet they are indispensable wilderness areas, if man, for whom we struggle, is also to have a refuge. We make refuges for ducks and geese, deer and elk, antelope and sage grouse. Man, too, needs places of retreat where once more he can embrace the wildness of the earth.

I read on and on through the hearings. I found some educators aligned with the commercial interests. A parent-teachers' association joined the alliance against this wildness. Why? Under federal law 25 per cent of all moneys received each year from a national forest, through timber sales or otherwise, is remitted to the state "for the benefit of the public schools and public roads of the county or counties in which such national forest is situated." The theory behind this law is that local governments should have compensation for the loss of income from taxation of land when the land is acquired by the federal government. Three national forests that touch the Chelan area have produced for the counties as much as one million dollars in one year.

Powerful voices are thus aligned against the wilderness areas. Those areas desperately need friends. These days people think more and more in terms of dollars. By those standards all of our wilderness will be chewed up by machines. Yet dollars do not express all the values which we Americans cherish.

I thought of the deep, quiet, fragrant forests beneath Glacier Peak that had never known the sounds of saws or axes—the cold, clear creeks draining land that had never experienced erosion—the trackless woods that had never heard the roar of automobiles—the sanctuaries in remote canyons never pierced by roads. I thought of the solitude of these places and the sacred quality of an undisturbed wilderness. An attempt to put dollar signs on these natural wonders is, I thought, a mark of our submission to the fleshpots, of our great decline. We deal with values that no dollars can measure. Glacier Peak nourishes restless man and helps keep him whole. This is a matter of the spirit beyond the expertise of appraisers of property.

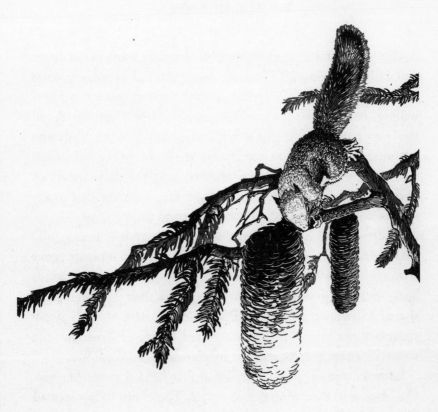

CHAPTER X

THE HIGH SIERRA

For height and for length, there are few wilderness areas that match the High Sierra. They are the rugged backbone of California. Their tree line at 11,000 feet reaches higher than most of our mountain ranges. Mount Whitney (14,495 feet) is taller than any of our peaks south of Alaska. Wind-swept ridges of the Sierra are as high as snow-clad Hood, Adams, and Rainier farther north. This is exhilarating country to travel. The air is thin. The peaks and canyon walls have colors of brilliant sunsets in them. It seems as if artistic hands mixed the pigments which they reflect.

One who climbs the great Sierra escarpment starts in the desert and ends in the Arctic. There are sagebrush and antelope ground squirrels in the desert valleys; and on the raw ridges is the dwarf willow, hardly four inches high, and the alpine chipmunk. In between are other life zones with trees and flowers, birds and mammals that exceed in variety those of any other wilderness area. The bright sunshine of Summer and the deep snows of Winter perform miracles with plant life, miracles that make species normally dull and monotonous vivid and exciting.

It seems as if I have known the Sierra all my life. I read John Muir when I was a boy, and through him came on intimate terms with this massive range. I was with him when the great winds blew and the pine and fir forests played their symphonies. I shared his winter exploits and alpine feats. Best of all, I knew from him the glories of the sculptured domes of Yosemite, the music of its waterfalls, and the brightness of its meadows.

Later I came to know Yosemite at first hand. I remember best Half Dome in a purplish sky at sunset. The entire valley seemed filled with mystery, and I felt a sense of excitement as I walked the trails. Earlier I had known the deep, dark, quiet forests of of the Coast Redwoods (*Sequoia sempervirens*). Those trees are the tallest living trees in the world, reaching as high as 364 feet. Their height and grandeur always seem to form for me a great cathedral of the woods. But they with all their glory had not fully prepared me for the stands of the giant sequoias (*Sequoia gigantea*), known as the Sierra Redwoods. This tree—the king of flora—has no equal. I first came to it from the western side, after climbing gentle slopes covered with live oaks and digger pines whose long, sparse needles give the tree a lacy appearance.

I found the Big Tree in groves that are as majestic as any crea- tion of the wilderness. These groves number some seventy, and are scattered over 250 miles of mountains. The patriarchs that they nourish were a thousand years old, or even more, when Christ walked Galilee. Their boles are so thick they would reach from curb to curb on a city street. Their limbs, which start a hundred feet or more from the ground, would be massive trees in their own right if stood on end. Some of these limbs at the tree trunk are six feet or more in diameter, and they often stretch out sixty or even seventy feet. A Big Tree that has not been marred by storms has a conical top. Many Big Trees, however, have met disaster in the several thousand years of their existence and show broken tops. Yet whether the crown is flat or pointed, each tree is a study in balance and harmony. Each is perfection on a massive scale.

The coast redwoods shut out most of the direct sunshine. But the Big Trees let the sunshine in; and the light shows these giants off in splendor. Their trunks are richly ruddy; their twigs and leaves a soft green. The sunshine that pours through makes every grove a bright temple. I like best the mixed groves, where other trees compete with the Big Tree. The ground cover is mountain misery—the leafy ground bramble that covers the shoes of a hiker with a resinous juice. Dogwood is the main understory—a tree whose white flowers brighten these temple woods in Spring. Bracken is here, too, and a sturdy ceanothus. But the attractions are upward, where the Big Trees reach up for blue sky. The Douglas squirrel includes the Big Tree in his domain. Mule deer walk quietly in the radiant light of this forest. Occasionally a coyote is seen. The main attraction, however, is always the Big Tree, whose stature makes men mute.

In these mixed woods the Big Tree has competition. The king of all pines, the sugar pine, grows here, and it is a worthy companion of the Big Tree. It rises 200 feet or more and has a girth of some thirty feet. Its trunk is a shaft of purplish brown, covered with yellowish lichens. The pileated woodpecker works loudly in its soft, light wood. The tree is slender and conical. No pine has a bole so clear of limbs. When the branches do appear, they extend forty feet or more. Its slender cones, which often are two feet long or even more, are the collector's item. Farther down the slopes on the western side stands the Douglas fir—superior in size to the sugar pine. But in the Big Tree groves the sugar pines tower above white firs, red firs, and red oaks that, in isolation, would be magnificent specimens in their own right.

This, then, was for years my conception of the Sierra. Yosemite and the western ridges and valleys represent an important segment of this Range of Light, as Muir liked to call these mountains. Yet they in all their glories are not the High Sierra.

The way I like to approach the high country is from the east. When I come from the west I climb gradually, the thick forest allowing only occasional glimpses of snowy crests. But when I arrive from the east I see the great escarpment and the soaring peaks for miles across the desert valleys of Nevada and California—an escarpment that is one of the geologic wonders of the world. When I reach the base, I look upward four or five thousand feet to the peaks. From Mono Lake a steep fault cliff rises abruptly 6000 feet to the mountain crest. From the little town of Lone Pine in Owens Valley I can see Whitney (and a number of other peaks only slightly lower) soaring two miles above the valley floor.

Most mountain ranges have their crest near their center. The Sierra is lopsided; its crest is at its eastern margin. To the west, it slopes gently to the Great Central Valley forty and fifty miles away. To the east it drops abruptly. As a table top would be tilted by lifting only one end, so did the Sierra rise along fractures or faults along its eastern edge.

Unlike the well-watered forests of the western slope, the eastern Sierra forests are sparse. For as the moisture-laden clouds from the Pacific billow upward to cross the gigantic Sierra barrier (whose lowest passes are 10,000 feet), most of their moisture falls on the western slope. The desert lands to the east are in the "rain shadow" of the Sierra.

When one travels from west to east over the Sierra, he comes to extensive stands of western white pine, the five-needle tree famous in the lumber history of the Pacific West. Its bark weathers to a silvery color. Its mature cones are reddish brown and up to eight or ten inches long. This tree that grows to over one hundred feet in height in the Sierra carries on the tradition of excellence which the eastern white pine of Maine represents. Its only equal in the field of soft wood is the sugar pine. Lower down on the east side of the Sierra is the Jeffrey pine. Those that first see the Jeffrey pine swear it is the ponderosa. Some botanists do indeed classify the two pines as one and the same thing. But on close examination the Jeffrey pine has distinct features. Its foliage is more blue-green than yellow-green. Its cones are larger and heavier, running up to eleven inches long; the prickles on these cones do not stand straight out as they do on the cone of the ponderosa but are backwardly hooked; and the Jeffrey cone has more of a purplish cast than a ponderosa cone. The Jeffrey cones are among the largest in the Pacific West and they are so handsome those who see them want to possess them.

One who drops off these eastern slopes in September and reaches the floor of the desert valley finds that it is streaked with yellow where the rabbitbrush is in bloom. But in April it is a riot of colors. Yellow arnica turns acres gold, and mixed with yellow is rose-pink, lavender, and white from a host of flowers that quickly bring a desert to life and as quickly vanish. Then the monotonous gray of bitter brush, sagebrush, and rabbitbrush return. The draws above the desert valley show aspen, mountain mahogany, and piñon pine. These, too, are mainly monotonous in color. But September is bright. Then the aspen forms golden plumes that make the canyons truly gay.

Snowbrush—a species of ceanothus named for David Douglas—fills these canyons with fragrance in early Summer. The wild roses run riot. The bright-yellow evening primrose flourish here. So do the cream-white mariposa lily and nude buckwheat. The yampa, sometimes known as wild caraway or Indian potato, displays small white flowers in umbrella-shaped clusters. This plant (which is quite palatable to stock) is kin to the Old World species that produces the caraway seed, and its tubers, which are sweet and nutty to the taste, were eaten by the Indians. Pennyroyal shows lavender flowers; forget-me-nots are sky blue; lupine is generously scattered.

Even in September, desert paintbrush is in bloom; the Bigelow sneezeweed is bright yellow; a few purple painted cups are still conspicuous, and the Pacific monardella—pinkish member of the mint family—nods gracefully. The green-leafed manzanita paints streaks of white across these canyon walls in June. Year round, its evergreen leaves, red-brown bark, and gnarled branches seem bright and gay.

These were a few of the choice discoveries Mercedes and I made one September when we went with Sierra Club friends up the canyon from Silver Lake to Agnew, Gem, and Waugh Lakes en route to the John Muir Trail. Here we also saw the juniper in new dimensions. This species of juniper is the same as the one in eastern Oregon. But it reaches more magnificent proportions

in the Sierra. It may live a thousand years or more. It seeks out isolated pinnacles or remote crags and there makes a stalwart stand. I had known it up north for its spindly branches that belly out into somewhat squat trees with sharp crowns. In the Sierra the crown is flat, the limbs few. The broad, flat top may, indeed, be as wide as the tree is high. The trunk is chunky, sometimes measuring over twenty feet in circumference. The limbs are gnarled and twisted—grotesquely shaped. The bark is a cinnamon red. The junipers in the canyons leading up to the High Sierra have visible root systems that are practically a duplicate of the tree itself. Large gnarled roots make sturdy loops over rocky outcrops and then strike down for water. Like the limbs above, they are twisted into fantastic shapes. *Juniperus occidentalis*—an excellent fence post in our country farther north—has a nobility of character in the High Sierra that places it in a select group of trees the world over.

The juniper is seldom found above 9000 feet. And only above 9000 feet does the High Sierra acquire its distinctive character.

This is vast, open country with long vistas that show distant peaks and ridges which lead one on and on through wind-blown passes and canyons filled with sapphire lakes. Lakes are everywhere—almost without number. They lie at the foot of talus slopes formed by avalanches, or in deep basins gouged out by glaciers, or in hollows dammed by glacial moraines. The signature of the glaciers is almost everywhere in the Sierra—on almost every lake shore, every headwall, every pass—for those who have eyes to see. There are rounded, ground-down ridges with parallel scratches indicating the direction of the ice movement; bathtub-sized grooves, mirror-smooth polished rock, as shining and fresh as if the glacier had melted away yesterday; boulders (up to truck size) carried several miles from their source.

There are sculptured walls like the ones in Yosemite. But they do not represent the High Sierra. This high, wind-swept country is more a land of sharp, broken ridges, penciled peaks, and bowl-like meadows. The rocks that decorate the skyline have a great variety of color and texture. Gerry Schumacher and his wife Genny explained the geology to us. On our trail from Rush Creek to McGee Pass, much of the rock we walked on and looked at is very, very old—so many millions of years old that one can only faintly comprehend such vast time. This ancient rock was born in a sea which once covered most of the West. Sediments that were deposited grain by grain formed layers of mud and gravel, the oldest being four hundred million years in age. Over and over, pressures and tensions from deep within the earth cracked them, tilted them, folded them, pushed them up into mountain ranges, and then submerged them below the sea again.

At last a great mass of molten granite welled up, shouldering aside some of the old rock, dissolving its way upward, squeezing into cracks and weak zones. This fluid mass never broke through the surface. It remained at great depth, cooling and solidifying over several million years. This is the light gray, crystalline mass that today forms most of the Sierra Nevada. Over a period of perhaps forty million years, water and weather eroded away the surface rock, finally uncovering the now solid granite. Today, in the great sea of Sierra granite, only island remnants of the old "mother rock" remain. Our trail followed some of the largest of those remnants.

Finally a great chunk of the earth's crust—a block 430 miles long and seventy miles wide—was gradually pushed upward along its eastern margin. As the Sierra was jerking upward, probably accompanied by thousands of intermittent earthquakes, the world's climate was cooling. Gradually the Ice Age set in—a million years when glaciers grew, melted back, then grew again—glaciers that at their height filled Sierra canyons with ice thousands of feet thick and spilled over the ridges until only the highest peaks remained ice-free. Only tiny, recent glaciers live in the Sierra today. They look like large snow fields. The huge glaciers of the Ice Age did not melt away perhaps until twelve thousand years ago.

In the central Sierra, shaped largely by fire and ice, the kinds and colors of rocks defy cataloging. Along the weakened, fractured zone of the great eastern Sierra fault, volcanic eruptions have flung showers of pumice and ash, and poured out great streams of lava. Red-cinder cones rise above Crater Meadows. Square miles of light-gray pumice are spread around Johnson Lake. There are glistening black basalt columns at Devil's Postpile. Lava ridges are dark gray or red. Other slopes are familiar granite. Some are almost white, polished by the glaciers so they gleam in the sunlight. In this setting the only relief is a green tree that cuts the reflection. Along Pine Creek and Upper Fish Creek dark metamorphosed rock shows spectacular intrusions of light-colored granite. Red Slate Mountain, which rises over 13,000 feet, is composed of old, sea-deposited rocks. They have many colors—red, green, and brown. Its slopes are difficult walking, and every step starts a movement of rocks that sound like music. Indeed they refer to these slate rocks as "musical glass." And when one climbs to McGee Pass (12,000 feet) that lies on the shoulder of Red Slate Mountain, he looks south into some of the wildest ridges there are in the world. Here is the northern Himalaya in duplicate. Deep canyons, sharp ridges, great vertical walls—all in black, white, red, blue-gray, rust, and brown—run riot. When clouds move in, these wild ridges take on new mystery. They are so rugged, so vast, so steep, they seem to be of another world.

Some of these ridges, once rich with grass, have been greatly depleted. The basin below McGee Pass was also heavily pounded by sheep—the animal Muir once called "the hoofed locust." It will take centuries to restore these high grasslands to the state they were in before the sheep ruined them.

There are enough high basins and ridges already ruined to make every oncoming generation vigilant, lest further depredations take place. But there are countless other meadows which have escaped the depredations of men who placed only a dollar sign on the wilderness. Tully Hole—just over the ridge from Virginia Lake and about 800 feet lower—and Horse Heaven, the next bench above it, are such places. They feed Fish Creek, one of the best trout streams in the Sierra. I could return to these meadows over and again without monotony. Neither is over forty acres in size, and each is rich in grass. They show a riot of color in early Summer. Even by Fall dark blue gentian and white columbine are in bloom. These meadows in September have the small yellow primrose and a bright yellow monkey flower on display. Red painted cups and the yellow hairy arnica are still in bloom. So is the diminutive Sierra penstemon. A prostrate lupine that has tiny gray leaves, a tiny spirea, and a dwarf mountain dandelion help make Tully Hole and Horse Heaven bright. A yellow bush cinquefoil lasts well into the Fall. A few bleeding hearts linger on. And in the rocky ledges that rim these basins are several different species of the goldenweed, sparkling bright and as sturdy as the white-bark pine that are the sentinels of this high country.

The wild onion (*Allium validum*) stands three feet high on a leafless triangular stalk and shows at the top a flat cluster of lavender flowers. This plant gives off the familiar onion odor, and, though stronger than the domestic onion, its stalk is an excellent ingredient for salads. This wild onion was one of my choice discoveries. Another was the high Sierra blueberry (*Vaccinium nivictum*) that bears tiny, sweet fruit and that is close kin to the dwarf blueberry we know further north, except that its leaves are green-blue, not bright green.

This, then, is Tully Hole and Horse Heaven—gouged out by glaciers, rimmed by polished granite and talus slopes, decorated by scatterings of whitebark pine, watered by fresh, cold streams, and colored by exotic flowers. Neither sheep nor man has ruined them, and with vigilance they can remain one of our true wilderness sanctuaries.

Ritter, Banner Peak, and the Minarets dominate the skyline of the central High Sierra. These are sharp-pointed, rugged peaks of metamorphosed rock that carry none of the polish of glaciers but hold it well in the canyons. Below them on the east lie numerous lakes. From any of these on a clear day are endless views of sapphire waters, whitebark pine, granite slopes, and ragged peaks. My favorite view is from the upper part of Thousand Island Lake, where Banner Peak seems to stand in isolation above a wide expanse of deep blue water. It carries several small glaciers in its hollows. It is as beautiful when reflected in the lake as it is on high. Ed and Peggy Wayburn sat with me in the shade of an ancient whitebark pine to watch it against a sky of fleecy clouds. There were frogs on the water's edge. A ruffed grouse went out at our approach. Clark's nutcrackers scolded from a treetop. A robin appeared, strangely silent. Mountain bluebirds dropped in for a brief visit. White-crowned sparrows swept the treetops in nervous flight. And then old friends from the north, Oregon juncos, moved in for a longer stay. Along the edges of the rocks grew the low-bush Sierra evergreen known as chinquapin. This plant (which has ill-smelling flowers) was now in fruit. Tiny burrs held a sweet kernel somewhat resembling a chestnut. (The origin of their botanical name is Castanopsis; and in Greek *kastanea* is chestnut and *opsis* is resemblance. This little Sierra species has a cousin in the Coast Range known as the giant chinquapin that grows up to fifty feet and, at places, to a hundred feet. It is heavily foliated with deep green leaves faced with gold and painted and curved in the lines of a pagoda.) When we passed by, fireweed and elephants' heads had passed their prime. The shooting stars had faded. Golden groundsel, with ragged yellow heads, still showed. Near me bloomed a lone buttercup.

The deep silence of the wilderness became profound. There was no sound to break it. It is then that men have reveries; mine carried me back to memories of how Banner Peak got its name. As Muir observed many years ago, snow crystals are driven by wind with such force as to become powder. When the Sierra wind moves from the northwest to north to clear the storms, the snowdust is whipped against the base of the mountain, sending it upward with a powerful thrust. When the snowdust reaches the top, the wind carries it south in a horizontal plane. Then is when snow banners are formed, some of them a half mile long. Snow banners fly from most Sierra peaks in winter. Banner Peak has the configuration that produces some of the most spectacular ones. Hence its name.

Banner Peak in Summer seems to follow me wherever I go in the central High Sierra. It has become for me an inseparable companion. It is my choice of all Sierra peaks.

Countless rock gardens, miniature in size, can be found in the High Sierra. Clear, quiet pools of icy water are rimmed by purple gentian. Some of the alpine slopes show white phlox and dwarf lavender asters. White heather—the cassiope that John Muir loved—runs riot. Yellow monkey flowers flourish; and tiny yellow daisies make a rockslide gay. And a minute paintbrush of deep red runs to the water's edge on some lakes.

The flower found highest of all is the Sierra polemonium. I picked it on McGee Pass. It is a small, bluish-purple flower more abundant than any other at these high altitudes. One who. finds it in the rocks at his feet knows he has reached a life zone where Summer is a very brief interlude. The climber puts it in his hat or her hair as a token of triumph. It symbolizes conquest and victory, though its pungent odor would seem to destine it for a lesser role.

Some well-watered slopes that run off the sharp ridges are almost jungles of wild flowers in July and August. The blazing star, with five yellow petals that are six inches across, stands knee-high. Red and yellow columbine grows very tall. Many plants stand as high as a man. That is true of white cow parsnip and swamp whiteheads. Orange tiger lilies tower above the average man. Dark blue monkshood and delphinium are six feet tall. Lavender lupine and wild onion, yellow senecio and red paintbrush will hide the average woman. Most spectacular of all are the corn lilies (false hellebore), whose yellowish spires rise seven feet. To those who come down from the north these seem to be Paul Bunyan flowers. Moist hillsides are indeed extravaganza in proportions that even Hollywood has not imagined. Soil, sunshine, and moisture combine to make record stands of flowers which farther north are diminutive.

The lakes of the High Sierra seem to be almost without number. They are sapphire blue; they lie between massive rock ridges, polished smooth by glaciers. There are trout in these lakes, some of them being the famed golden trout whose underbody shows the brilliance of sunsets when they are first removed from water. Occasional gulls put themselves down in these waters. Water ouzels—who have an oil gland ten times larger than that of related land birds—use the streams that flow into those lakes or out of them as their feeding grounds. They dive into white water and work over the rocks under plunging, foaming streams. They sing their hearts out even in the meanest weather and make the weariest traveler feel renewed.

The High Sierra shows lodgepole pine—an old friend from the Cascades and Wallowas—in new proportions. It grows to greater thickness here than it does up north. And its Sierra environment gives its bark a dark orange hue that makes it much gayer than its northern kin. Up north it often grows as thick as hair on a dog. Groves of these spindly trees—some dead but still standing—are indeed so dense up north as to become difficult to traverse by one going cross-country. Yet north or south, some of the cones often remain on the trees unopened for many years. When a fire comes, the holocaust among lodgepole is severe. But the seeds, protected by thick resin, survive; and a new forest of lodgepole springs up. Thus does this tree thrive on disaster. Moreover it is a pioneer tree that moves in where lumbering has leveled an ancient forest. And in the Sierra, as elsewhere, this indomitable lodgepole slowly encircles open meadows when the water table falls (as it does if there is overgrazing) and gradually invades them. There are Sierra meadows that in another century will be thick lodgepole groves, ecologists say, unless man or disaster intervenes.

The lodgepole gains in size and stature in the Sierra due in part to the great snowfall. Roughly speaking, there is at lower altitudes an addition of 200 inches of snow for every 1000 feet of elevation. Above 6500 feet the volume of snow decreases. Yet even at the higher altitudes it is bountiful. The 10,000-foot meadows we crossed might have thirty feet of snow before next Summer. That is the average snowfall. Records of sixty feet are not uncommon. The snow lies flat, hanging on until early Summer. It does not rush madly off. It melts slowly into the soil, nourishing the trees. It is deep, warm, life-giving snow. It protects the vegetation of the high basins from the icy blasts that cut across the higher ridges. The greatness of the Sierra trees is due in large measure to it.

Whitebark pine—that starts around 9500 feet, marks the tree line at 11,000 feet, and is found at 12,000 feet or higher—is more familiar to one who comes down from the north. Sometimes its bark, lashed by fierce winds and cut by blasts of sand, is reddish silver. It survives under great adversity; and the icy forces that oppose it give it nobility in appearance, though it be twisted or stunted or eccentrically deformed. I recall one that Dave Brower and I found not far from McGee Lake. It may well have been 1000 years old. Its main stem stood thirty feet high, and at first glance it seemed dead and wasted. But on the far side younger sprouts from the taproot were flourishing. They probably were several centuries old and would carry the old tree through perhaps another millennium.

Whitebark pine fringes high meadows of the Sierra where a low lupine, the bright white heather, and the heather with a magenta hue take hold. A dwarf willow only inches high also grows here, and by September shows its fuzzy catkins. Deep blue gentian linger on as bright reminders of meadows gaily painted during summer months. And there is a special reward to one who travels this trail in early Fall and drops to his knees to learn the mysteries of these rich alpine lawns. Deep in the grass is the delicate white gentian, still fresh and gay. The shore lines of the lakes also show these bright gentians. Here, too, are Labrador tea and the bog laurel, whose pink blossoms are among the first to bloom after the snow recedes. A "gooseberry currant" with stiff yellow spines shows its tart fruit by late August. A cousin of the green-leafed manzanita runs in carpets along rocky slopes. By September the High Sierra blueberry that grows close to the ground has turned from green to yellow to red. Whole hillsides are so saturated with its rich crimson that, as Mercedes put it, the High Sierra has the touch of New England on it.

Some ridges have mountain hemlock on one slope and red firs (*Abies magnifica*) on another. The mountain hemlock grows to magnificent proportions above 9500 feet, flourishing on the cold north slopes or in shaded areas. From a distance its drooping branches and its drooping tip give it a sad appearance. But at closer range it has dignity and grace. The cones that lie at its feet mark it as the perfect craftsman. For each one is precision made—a tiny replica of a stately conifer.

The red firs prefer the sunny slopes. Their bark is often six inches thick, and their red-brown color and massive size mark them as patriarchs of the High Sierra. They grow over 200 feet high and up to five feet in diameter. Their bark is indeed rich in color. Their lower branches sweep down; the upper ones are lifted to the skies. There is beauty, grace, and splendor in this tree. I experienced a thrill when I saw them—and I softly whistled, as I did when I first saw the Cedars of Lebanon and the great deodars of the Himalayas. One who sees this deep red bark and the massive stance of the red fir in the High Sierra will never forget the tree. The eight-inch cones stand upright on the top branches and weigh up to a half pound; each one is streaked with fresh balsam.

We had entered great red-fir groves after climbing the ridge out of Shadow Lake, which now lay in purple splendor below us. A series of other lakes followed, each one a distinct personality, each a quiet, exquisite alcove in a harassed world. These are places of magnificence to camp for a week or more. This day, however, we pushed on, taking the trail that swings down pumice slopes to Johnson Lake, which lies at 8500 feet. Here the ferns are lush. False hellebore, long past its prime, showed dry husks. The little tiger lily, which stood six feet high, was now in seed. Larkspur as tall as a man and monkshood of equal size were now only dry stalks. Beyond Johnson Lake I found several species of lupine, all in pod and some waist-high. Pennyroyal still showed some of its lavender flowers. I had not gone far before I came to some magnificent red firs, where I stopped to rest.

A Belding ground squirrel was the first to challenge my presence. This small yellowish-brown creature first popped up behind a fallen tree and stood perfectly still, his forelegs pressed closely to his chest. Then he made a short, whistling call and melted to the ground. Up he came again with his whistling sound, only to disappear again. Perhaps there were several in the group who were inspecting me. In any case there was always one popping up behind the log, standing perfectly still, and then mysteriously disappearing with a warning whistle.

There was a greater disturbance high above me in the fir trees. Down came two Douglas squirrels to protect their sovereignty over this domain. They are small squirrels about a foot long, their tails being two thirds the size of their bodies. They are brownish gray on top and buff underneath. Their bright eyes and long black whiskers give them a fierce look. They have been called the squirrel of squirrels by reason of their quick nervous actions and their easy, flashing movements. The two who came down to assert their dominion against my invasion fairly raced around the trunk of the tree, making a giddy pattern as they darted up and down, around and around, all the while punctuating their frenzied action with dots and exclamation points of frozen positions. Perhaps they were only investigating me. In any case, after shouting "chee-up, chee-up" many times, they soon raced up the fir tree overhead; and I could hear their sharp ivory scissors working furiously in the treetop. Soon a missile landed at my side, barely missing my head. It was a huge red-fir cone. I started to reach for it, when another came whistling down. I had not retrieved the first when a third landed with a thud. I was being bombarded from on high, and these bombardiers were experts. I quickly retreated and, finding an open knoll, stood and watched my newly found friends at work. They raced along branches where the cones stood upright, not pausing for breath after finishing one job and before starting another. The cones came down like huge hailstones, each landing with an ominous thud. Soon the cone cutters came down the tree to process the cones that had fallen. Though each cone was twice as heavy as the squirrel, that seemed to present no problem. The squirrels dragged the cones to the foot of the tree with their teeth, each managing one without difficulty. Then, turning the cones bottom side up, they demolished them, peeling off each layer of spiraling husks. Though the cones were tightly sealed, the Douglas squirrels opened them more deftly than a man could have done with a knife. Husk after husk dropped before any dark-reddish seeds with rose-red wings were found. Some of the seeds were eaten. Others were carefully harvested and buried in underground storehouses for winter fare. These industrious friends of mine seemed to me to be the busiest, most efficient animal of the woods. Clark's nutcrackers dropped down to share the feast of the red fir seeds. But my friends savagely chased them away. A Belding ground squirrel received the same treatment. The Douglas squirrel seemed to me at that moment to be the king of the High Sierra. He is, indeed, almost supreme. A hawk occasionally kills one. So does a bobcat. But I was to learn that the most relentless enemy of all is the pine marten, who can match the Douglas squirrel in speed and agility even in the highest tree.

My visit with the Douglas squirrel carried me back again to John Muir, who had popularized this squirrel of squirrels. I thought of the crusade he carried on to preserve this area as a wilderness. His ideas of conservation eventually were reflected in our federal laws.

The case for federal regulation of forest lands was dramatized in the early history of the Sierra. Sheep pounded ridges and valleys to dust, and reckless forestry practices devastated large areas. The damage done by utility companies is still evident. Agnew and Gem, two choice lakes in the eastern side, were made into reservoirs for hydroelectric power, and Rush Meadows was flooded to make Waugh Lake. One who hikes that region in the Fall can see how the power project has turned Waugh, the highest of these lakes, into an ugly pond.

This High Sierra country is now in four national parks and about eight national forests. The parks are more secure sanctuaries than the forests, since the sheep and cattlemen and the lumbermen have no claim on them. Forest lands, too, can be classified as wilderness areas and thus become sanctuaries where commercial interests cannot intrude. The struggle in the Sierra, as elsewhere, is to get more of the unclassified lands classified as wilderness areas.

Today, however, the greatest Sierra threat is in the clamor for more highways.

Seven main arteries carry traffic over the Sierra. Yet, as I write, the pressure for another road is mounting. A small but loud Chamber of Commerce is blowing its horn. Others who want to commercialize the High Sierra are joining those ranks.

California's population is 15 million today, and it will certainly be at least double that by the end of this century. That means greater and greater pressure on these inner meadows. The bald truth is that these high lakes and basins will not survive that mounting use if they are made more readily accessible. Today they are subject to nearly the maximum pressure they can stand, even when access is restricted to those who come on foot or by horse. Garnet Lake, a deep blue gem at the base of Banner Peak, had 1000 visitors this last August. Garnet Lake, happily, has no road. One reaches it from road's end only after half a day's hiking. Yet the traffic into it is so great today that the problems of sanitation and wood supply become considerable. Other lakes are sorely pressed. Their condition is illustrated by what two Sierra Club members, Anne and Fred Eissler, recently discovered. From the shores of four lakes (that can be reached only by horse or on foot) they collected three and a half tons of tin cans—and packed them out. Three and a half tons of tin cans represented only two or three summers of use. But those tons of tin cans emphasize how heavy the traffic is. More roads mean heavier and heavier use, and heavier use means the ultimate destruction of these wilderness sanctuaries. They are fragile creations. The soil is thin; the timber is limited; the water supply is easily polluted; the growing season is short.

The day is not far distant when permits to camp at Garnet Lake or any of the other camp sites in the High Sierra may have to be obtained. They will be restricted in number to save these high basins from being pounded to dust by the feet of men and horses. This must be done if those yet unborn are to know the High Sierra as wilderness. More roads mean a shrinking wilderness. Yet an increasing population indicates that our goal should be an expanding wilderness, even if we must put stumps and worn-out lands in parks or forests and over the next century develop them as sanctuaries.

I always hate to leave the Sierra. I get a strange exhilaration there. I want to go on and on, whether horseback or on foot, climbing the next pass and discovering the mysteries of the next valley. This is wind-blown country that charms the traveler and makes him captive. Only great compulsions, such as Robert Frost wrote about, bring me down:

> The woods are lovely, dark and deep,
> But I have promises to keep,
> And miles to go before I sleep,
> And miles to go before I sleep.

I had seen a sun set over Banner Peak that turned clouds lavender and gold and red. I had felt the sting of sleet in high meadows and had heard gentle rain on my Himalayan tent at night. There was no sun this last morning, as a snowstorm was gathering over McGee Pass. The aspen was turning from yellow to red as I dropped down the canyon below McGee Lake. A Townsend solitaire sang its song in a stand of lodgepole pine. Its song, infinitely sweet, was filled with runs and trills that died away only to resurge again and, finally, to fade into plaintive whispers.

Beavers were busy in the creek. Mountain quail were in great abundance. The bark of the water birch showed copper even on this gray day. Mist hung over the barren peaks that dominate this canyon. But once in a while the wind lifted the curtain and showed startling walls of red rock mixed with white rock.

When I reached the road's end, I was still 8000 feet above sea level. As I turned to have a last look at the high country that claims much of my heart, the clouds parted. There in brilliance stood the peaks that guard the high basins, and as quickly as they appeared, they vanished. Dark clouds swallowed the High Sierra, though I was in warm sunshine. I silently thanked Muir for introducing me to these peaks of mystery and beauty. I knew then that his fight—which was partially lost at the hands of those who value wilderness only in terms of dollars—was an unending one. All who love the wilderness for the spiritual values it represents must now close ranks if we are to have even small islands of it to bequeath to those who are to follow.

CHAPTER XI

WALLOWAS

Whenever I sleep out in the Wallowas, I keep one ear cocked for the midnight sounds of the porcupine. They often come to camp in the dead of night to chew on saddles, reins, or bridles which can be reached tiptoe.

The porcupine is a mammal whose young is born in late May or early June. It shuns the dense conifer forest and seeks out the more open areas. In the Summer it feeds primarily on herbs and bushes. In the Winter its food is primarily tree-gathered. It is fond of pine needles and pine bark, especially the ponderosa. It strips the bark, eating almost exclusively the cambium and phloem layers. This is, in large part, its winter food. This girdling causes the tree to die. In some areas of the Pacific West the porcupine's depredations, particularly of ponderosa pine, have been so severe that programs of reforestation have been defeated. A porcupine will girdle even the smallest tree, for it needs only a pine that is one inch in diameter to have a winter feast.

These awkward, waddling animals are so slow on foot they can be killed with a club. To dogs, however, they present a formidable array of quills. There are some 30,000 on each porcupine. Each quill is detachable, and the porcupine uses its tail to drive them into the face of an attacking animal. The coyote, too, can be a victim of the porcupine. But age-old experience has taught it to be cautious, and its innate cunning has led it to devise clever ways of dealing with this opponent.

The coyote's littering months are in late Spring—April and May. By July the parents are giving them their first lessons in catching game. They start with mice, rats, and rabbits. The lessons also include the porcupine, as I learned one July day as I headed up the Minam River.

The Wallowas (which lies in Oregon at the corner where that state touches Washington and Idaho) are shaped like a huge wagon wheel, Eagle Cap being the hub and the Lostine and Minam canyons being two of the spokes. The North Minam Meadows is near the headwaters of the North Fork of the Minam River. It is where the grass is lush, the red fir magnificent, the rainbow trout brilliant. The late Roy Schaeffer, my companion along many wilderness trails, lived on the Lostine. The quickest route from his place to the North Minam Meadows is cross-country over a tumble of granite ridges. But this July the snow still lay in deep drifts along the high trail. So Roy and I took the long way around, going to the mouth of the Minam Canyon and then traveling horseback up that open, hospitable canyon where pine, fir, and tamarack flourish. We had not gone far when we saw the remains of a porcupinie freshly killed and many signs of coyote tracks circling the corpse. We had just missed a seminar on how a coyote kills a porcupine. Roy, drawing on his experiences, filled in the details.

A coyote circled this porcupine, going round and round. The pups sat on a ledge watching the performance. The mother circled first one way then another, and then back again. Once in a while she would pretend to charge the porcupine. But she took pains to keep out of range of his quills. How long these tactics of badgering the porcupine went on we do not know. Roy said a coyote sometimes circled, charged, retreated, and then circled again for several hours. The game was to get the porcupine angry enough to stand up on its hind legs. Then the soft underbelly would be exposed. The coyote was patient and persistent, waiting until the porcupine reared. In that instant the coyote charged, and its sharp teeth sank into the porcupine's belly. A neat peeling back of the skin followed, and then the pups were called in for the feast.

Roy and I talked of the coyote and its place in nature's scheme of things. The coyote is despised by sheepmen, whose flocks graze the Wallowas. I recalled John Muir's saying, "They are beautiful animals, and, although cursed of man, are loved of God. Their sole fault is that they are fond of mutton." Roy despised the coyote for its depredations on deer.

The coyote takes a few fawns but is seldom a match for mature deer except when snow is on the ground. Even then, the deer can usually make a getaway. But when the crust that comes in dead of winter is heavy enough to hold up a coyote but too light for a deer, the coyotes make their deer kills.

Government men once used the venomous 1080 (wartime code for sodium fluoro-acetate) in the Wallowas to control the coyote. It killed that animal, but it also killed all the others that took the same bait or that ate off the carcass of one who had. Birds as well as rodents were destroyed. Nature's nice balance was upset. Today that balance has been largely restored. Cougars, coyotes, and men take their annual harvest of deer and elk. But the population of these animals is on an upward trend, though the hunters are also increasing. Only about sixty per cent of people hunting deer with rifles make a kill. In the case of elk, the percentage is about eighteen.

One who travels the canyons of the Wallowas in Summer will see many deer. The elk, too, are abundant, but by late June they are high under the snow fields. Summer forage is in good supply. The only problem is with winter forage. Deer in eastern Oregon have known disastrous Winters. There have been some notorious "crashes" in deer population, due to starvation. But as this is written the delicate balance is being well maintained—thanks, in part, to the coyote.

This trail up the Minam winds over forty miles through a canyon that is never more than a half mile wide. The central core of the Wallowas and their main ridges are granite. But much of the Minam is lava rock. Several layers can be seen on the canyon walls that rise two thousand feet above the river. The lava sometimes makes out into bald buttes, sometimes into cliffs flanked by grassy slopes. There is timber to the top; but the most prized trees are in the valley. Yellow-bellied ponderosa pine are ancient monarchs. Red fir, thinly scattered, is usually a magnificent specimen. White pine is also a patriarch. Some stretches of this canyon are like a park. The understory in the lower reaches is the ever-green—kinnikinnick—that covers the ground like a mat. Bracken, snowberry, blackberries, currants, and blueberries are scattered. Willow, alder, and hawthorn grow close to the river. In June this canyon is ablaze with wild flowers. By late July even the wild roses and wild strawberries have passed, and the lupine is in pod. But the gay cinquefoil is in bloom. Purple thistle and white clover fringe the trail. There are patches of the lovely catchfly that opens by day and closes by night. And the ocean spray, our most abundant flowering shrub in the West, leaves touches of white on the hillsides. Higher up the slopes is the snowbrush that fills the canyon with its fragrant perfume in June. When one has traveled fifteen miles or more up the canyon, the tamarack appear. Blueberries, snowberries, and bracken grow thicker. But the most conspicuous ground cover then is the dainty twinflower—the favorite plant of the great Linnaeus. This woody vine is an evergreen that sends up slender stems a couple of inches high from which two tiny pink bells are suspended. Their fragrance is haunting; they are delicate creations to find in forests of towering trees and huge granite boulders sitting on lava rock. Another delicate creation often grows with the twinflower. This is the coolwort foam flower, whose tiny white flowers circle a tall stem that stands a foot above the forest floor. There are also wild geranium in bloom in July, and once when I stopped for lunch by a cold tributary of the Minam River, I discovered that I had two bright companions. They were a pair of sego lilies—white petals gracefully cupped and wearing a purplish pit above the sepal.

The river itself is as charming as any of the beauties that surround it. The water is cold and clear and every half mile or so a tumbling tributary feeds it. The water seems clearer than any American stream I have seen. A chemical analysis might disprove my boast. It may be that the bright granite rocks and the gleaming white sand which make up the river bed give the water its unusual clarity. I do know from years of camping there that the Minam offers the most delicate fishing of any mountain stream we have. The cold water is ideal for rainbow trout, and three-foot salmon come all the way from the Pacific to spawn there in July. One has to use great care to catch these fish. The only sure way is to fish upstream, touching a pool or the calm water below a riffle once or twice with a fly and then moving on. My favorite site for camping is Granite Crossing, some twenty-three miles up the river. There is a small falls near there, and the late Blaine Hallock taught me how to fish it. The time was dawn; the fly was dry. The cast was just below white water. The first cast always brought a twelve- or fourteen-inch rainbow to net. Then Blaine would leave the water and rest under a fir tree for five minutes by his watch. The next cast in the same spot always brought another rainbow. Then he would rest five minutes, and so on. The rest periods gave the pool a chance to settle down and get over its excitement. Those who whip the Minam never have luck.

The Minam is a valley fragrant with balsam. When I walk it or ride it horseback I breathe deep, for the essence of pine and fir is in the air. This fragrance may have some relation to temperature and humidity. The air is dry; the days are warm. The lava rock overhead collects and retains heat; and the valley is just under the 4000 foot level. The fragrance may be due to other causes which I do not know. My experience is not unique; all who travel the canyon talk about it. And on my last trip there I learned that this priceless pine and fir are in jeopardy. I stayed with Red Higgins, who has a guest ranch near the fifteen-mile post. I learned that night that the Forest Service plans to let lumber operators cut some twenty miles of the Minam River Canyon. Many excuses were tendered. One was that a road was necessary in order to take men quickly into good fishing grounds. Another was that if the big game of the Wallowas are to be harvested, trucks and pickups should be able to go deep into the mountains. These reasons are specious. Fishing can never be good on a stream like the Minam, if any car can reach it. When trucks can get to the heart of the Wallowas, the big game will be on the way out. Fishing on these small streams, like hunting in the basins, can be good only so long as extra effort is needed to get there. The value of roadless areas is partly in the rewards which are at trail's end. When roads supplant trails, the precious, unique values of God's wilderness disappear.

This passion for roads is partial evidence of our great decline as a people. Without effort, struggle, and exertion, even high rewards turn to ashes. There is no possible way to open roadless areas to cars and retain a wilderness. This is one diabolic consequence of the "multiple use" concept as applied. The Forest Service recognizes, of course, that application of the "multiple use" principle means that some areas must be devoted exclusively or predominantly to a single purpose. The difficulty is that, in the Pacific West, "multiple use" in practical operation means that every canyon is usually put to as many uses as possible—lumber operations, roads, campsites, shelters, toilets, fireplaces, parking lots, and so on.

There are of course many who can get close to forests only by automobiles. Not everyone has the legs or the lungs to venture to the interior on his own. Recreational facilities must be provided for them. But once the interior is tapped by roads, the wilderness is gone forever. Lumbering and real wilderness, motoring and real wilderness, hotels and real wilderness are mutually exclusive. The choice must be made. If there is to be a true wilderness in the Wallowas where trees are thick, where the valley is fragrant with balsam, where the canyon is filled only with the murmur of pine and fir and with the whispering of water, roads must be kept out. The bits of wilderness left to us are only tiny islands. The Minam River is one. Turning it over to the lumber interests for cutting and road building would be a reckless act taken in defiance of the wondrous creations God has placed there. It would be as much a desecration as the destruction of the mighty cathedrals created by the sequoias in California. It would be another sign that the dollar leads our civilization, that for man's nobler side we leave but a few crumbs.

Some of the Wallowas are technically a wilderness area. But its boundaries follow mostly the contours of the high country. The rich tongues of forested lands that stretch up the canyons are outside the wilderness areas. They are left outside on purpose, so that lumber mills may move in. Indeed what is within or without a wilderness area is determined by the fiat of the Secretary of Agriculture on the recommendation of the Chief Forester. Neither of these men is elected by the people; each is beyond the electoral will. Moreover, "the law" under which they act is a set of regulations which they themselves drew. They can revise those regulations at will. Acts of Congress can be repealed or revised on a vote of those whom the people have chosen to be their representatives. But the question whether new land shall be put in a wilderness or whether land presently included should be taken out or, in truth, whether we shall have any wilderness areas at all is resolved exclusively within the hierarchy of a federal bureaucracy. A Forest Service man with wilderness values paramount in his thinking will protect these sanctuaries and add to them. One who at heart is closer in tune with lumber and mining interests will narrow these corridors and let commercial interests have their way. Whether we have more or fewer wilderness areas depends therefore on the chancy circumstances as to what men reach the top in the federal bureaucracy. Great issues of social security, power dams, reclamation, soil conservation, price controls, quotas for farmers, and the like are debated in Congress. Yet the issue of whether the people will be left a rich wilderness area or a dust bowl of stumps, serviced by roads, is left to the whim or caprice of a bureaucrat. If the Minam is to be ravished, if roads are to pierce this wilderness, the people should decide it after fair debate. It is their inheritance that is at stake. God made it, and it is among the loveliest of His creations. If it is to be protected, changes in the basic law governing national forests must be made. These sanctuaries need the mantle of protection that only an Act of Congress can give them.

This is what we said at Red Higgins' ranch as the sun set over the western ridge and started the sundial moving up the opposite canyon wall. A kingfisher cried noisily as it streaked across the water. Two grosbeaks whirled and turned in the air as they dived on insects. The soft murmur of the river was drowned out when a cool wind swept up the canyon and made the conifers sing. Then the clear voice of the willow thrush came floating from a cottonwood—"vee-ur, vee-ur, veer, veer." All this was music sweeter by far than screeching saws cutting through trees, the crash of timbers, or the roar of automobile traffic in this wilderness retreat.

The top country of the Wallowas also has its special claims. The granite ridges are knife-edged. The talus slopes are so numerous that the traveler has to pick with care his route to the top. Above 5000 feet the alpine fir is the dominant tree. They march in stately fashion up the canyon walls, skirting rockslides and granite cliffs. Some Englemann's spruce march with them. But when the tree line is passed at 9000 feet, the last tree seen is the whitebark pine. Ancient patriarchs, long dead, mark some ridges. For decades on end they stand erect even after life has passed. The live ones are bent, gnarled and dwarfed. Snow is not off these ridges for more than three months each year. Winters are severe, and the icy blasts that whirl across these mountains are great levelers. Only the whitebark pine survives, the one tree of our western mountains that seems to thrive on adversity.

Those high ridges once had grass, knee-high. Reckless sheepmen and easygoing rangers of the Forest Service allowed them to be denuded by overgrazing. Now they are mostly coarse sand. When I see these barren ridges I remember John Muir's saying, "When sheep advance, flowers, vegetation, grass, soil, plenty, and poetry vanish." Tiny saxifrage are slowly taking hold. Mats of white and pink phlox are expanding. Yellow cushion eriogonum dot some of the bleak, bare places. Occasionally the bright snow buttercup is there to lift the heart.

When the snow first goes off the lake basins and the bunch grass is beginning to recover from the great weight of the snow, there are wonders to behold. The pink heather and the cerise paintbrush are among the first to bloom. The tiny blue alpine speedwell—excellent for salads—seems positively gay. Then is the time when some drab meadows are brought to life by a dark, dark blue penstemon. Labrador tea blooms early. And perhaps the choicest reward of all is the monkey flower—rich purplish-red and a noble bouquet for any lake's edge.

There are over a hundred lakes in the Wallowas. Probably all have not yet been discovered. Some are not yet named. Each has a distinct personality.

Some, like New Deal, rest in treeless basins. Mud Lake is a tiny pocket on a steep slope. Cheval is a deep hole at the end of a great talus slope—large enough to accommodate only one party. Douglas is rimmed by granite spires. Bumble, Patsie, and Tombstone are like ponds in friendly pastures. Diamond, Frances, and Lee have the look of wells without bottoms and icy water that chills to the marrow. Green, Minam, and Crescent are rich with algae. Blue and Chimney show clayish bottoms and have a sterile look. Hobo has golden trout. Long—noted for rainbows—is a wide expanse that shows whitecaps on windy days. Swamp—filled with golden trout—lies in a large basin, rimmed by slopes that show countless rockslides and decorated by ancient and elegant whitebark pine.

But my favorite of all is Steamboat, out of which the North Fork of the Minam rises. It is rimmed by talus slopes and by granite walls highly polished by glaciers. Alpine fir has taken hold in many spots. Whitebark pine and Englemann's spruce compete for second place. A meadow of ten or twenty acres fills one end of this basin. The lake occupies the rest, creating the impression that it rests in a large saucer that is about to spill over at one end. Polished-granite ledges run at a gentle slope into the sapphire-blue water, where eastern brook trout live. This is a fly fisherman's paradise. High benches are ablaze with the tiny purple bush penstemon. The lake's edge is gay with the pinkish, waxy flowers of the pyrola. My camp is not in the meadows but in a small cluster of conifers at the opposite end. An ice-cold stream hardly a foot wide runs on the edge of these trees. It has a white, sandy bottom and is excellent refrigeration for food. One sits on top of the world at Steamboat Lake. The nights are crisp; the dawn is fresh with dew. This is a world unto itself, untouched by civilization, unspoiled by man.

My daughter, Millie, had a horse, Lightning, that could go cross-country in the roughest terrain. I used to ride him, leaving the trail and heading up steep slopes looking for lakes under high peaks. The canyons are the home of the ruffed grouse and Franklin's fool hens. The higher slopes Lightning and I crossed are the habitat of the blue grouse. Here on slopes of pine grass under Douglas fir we would find great coveys. And on the talus slopes we skirted I got to know the conies well. These conies, sometimes known as pikas, are scattered throughout the Wallowas. Their sharp, short call, "eek, eek," carries a long distance. Conies are guinea-pig size, and in the Wallowas they are dark reddish brown. Their legs are short and the soles of their feet are furred. The tail is merely a tuft of white. They live in rockslides that give them protection from most of the predators. In the Wallowas the marten hunts them the year round, and the coyotes and hawks stalk them when the snow is off. These conies live on grasses, vines, shrubs, and most of the wild flowers. They love lupine. They collect bundles of these products and spread them out in the sun to dry. If a storm comes, they collect the hay and put it underground and then lay it out again for curing when the sun shines. When the grasses and stalks are cured, they store them in the rocks for winter use. It's not unusual to find fifty pounds of perfectly cured hay under a cony's rockslide.

Lightning and I found lakes that others have missed. We camped in high meadows where Scotch bluebells were waist-high. We knew hot days. We knew bright days with cooling winds, and rainy days when sleet swept the ridges, making my jacket stiff with ice.

Lightning was a versatile horse. He seldom refused a hazard. The North Minam River in June was often in flood, more than eight feet deep. But it presented no special problem to Lightning.

He swam the river, while my feet rested on his withers and the water washed the seat of my saddle. Going uphill with Lightning underneath was a rare experience. He seemed to enjoy the climb. All I need do was point his head to the top I wanted to reach and he picked the best way up. He stopped for breath when he desired. But his stops were not frequent. He always seemed in a hurry to reach the crest of the ridge; when he got there he always stopped, blew his nose, and looked around as if to say, "What a beautiful view."

Going downhill astride Lightning was also a treat. He had an easy swing in his joints that took out all the jar. When we came to a ledge he would jump down as nimbly as a cat. Two-foot cliffs, three-foot cliffs, four-foot cliffs—these he negotiated without any hesitation. Once on a cross-country trip from Steamboat Lake to the Lostine we came to a cliff that had a six-foot drop. This was the first and only time Lightning refused me. I dismounted, walked around the cliff, and stood at its base. At my command he jumped, and then waited for me to remount.

He was a nondescript horse who could produce no papers showing a pedigree. But he had inherited from distant sires the blood of champions that produced a horse as gentle and as adventuresome as any I ever knew. Lightning was a true aristocrat.

One day we topped the rugged ridge overlooking the North Minam Meadows on the west and mostly slid down the loose slopes until we reached a stand of quaking aspen, where the horsemint was lush. The flowering shrubs—serviceberry, chokeberry, red willow, elderberry, Labrador tea, and snowbrush—had passed their bloom. The fireweed was gay. The Scotch bluebells were still in flower. There were forget-me-nots on this slope. In a wet spot we came across a lovely yellow monkey flower. Here were monkshood, whose rich blue petals brightened the granite rocks. Cinquefoil nodded gracefully. Streaks of cotton grass showed below us. But the choice prize of all was Menzies' beard-tongue penstemon. The bluish-pink tubular flowers were fully two inches long. Dozens upon dozens were in bloom. The two upper lips and the three lower lips seemed as delicate as any membrane created. These lovely creations that thrive in meager soil and harsh conditions refuse to be transplanted even where soils are fertile. They belong exclusively to the high mountains. And so, in large part, does man, I thought.

Below me lay the North Minam Meadows, where grass is knee high. Clumps of alpine fir are scattered here and there. But for a mile or so the meadows have an open effect. The stream—filled with rainbow—meanders. This day the wind was blowing; and as the grass bowed before it, it looked silky. These meadows are, to those who know them, probably the most coveted of any in the land. The grass will hold horses for weeks on end. The water is cold and clear. Deer frequent the place. In early Summer bull elk make it their headquarters. The mile-high elevation makes the air light and bracing. Red fir, alpine fir, jack pine, Englemann's spruce make this their home. The mornings are fresh, and it takes the sun several hours to creep down the western wall. The evenings are cool and a chill settles over the meadows before the shadow creeps up the eastern wall.

This day Lightning and I were still in sunshine when the sun left the valley. Now the shadow passed us on its way up. The meadows at my feet were no longer sharp in detail. They took on an air of mystery. Then above me came the sweetest song I know. Audubon's hermit thrush sang over and over again. Its music is to me a haunting melody. It means the Wallowas, and lengthening shadows, and a sanctuary that greedy man must never destroy.

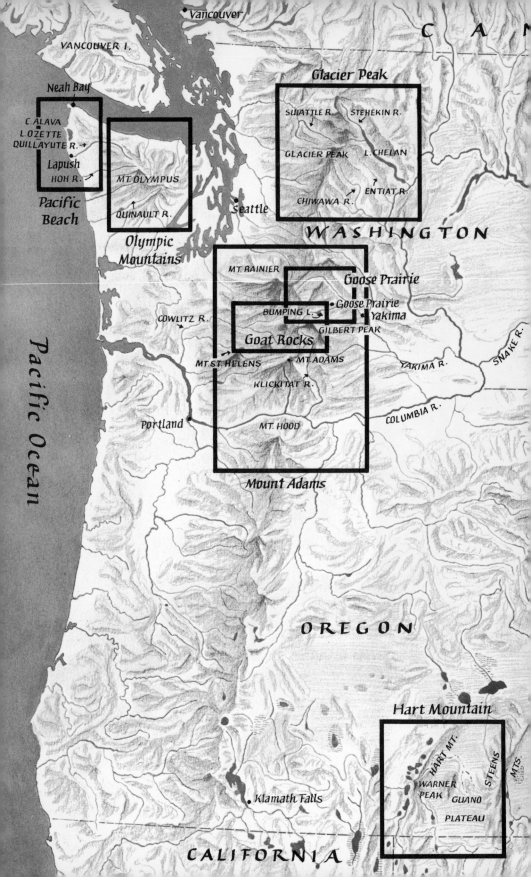

Vancouver

VANCOUVER I.

Neah Bay

C. ALAVA
L. OZETTE
QUILLAYUTE R.

Lapush

HOH R.

Pacific
Beach

MT. OLYMPUS

QUINAULT R.

Olympic
Mountains

Seattle

Glacier Peak

SUIATTLE R.   STEHEKIN R.

GLACIER PEAK   L. CHELAN

CHIWAWA R.   ENTIAT R.

WASHINGTON

MT. RAINIER

Goose Prairie

BUMPING L.   Goose Prairie
Yakima

COWLITZ R.   GILBERT PEAK

Goat Rocks

MT. ST. HELENS   MT. ADAMS

KLICKITAT R.   YAKIMA R.   SNAKE R.

Portland   MT. HOOD   COLUMBIA R.

Mount Adams

Pacific
Ocean

OREGON

Hart Mountain

HART MT.

STEENS
WARNER
PEAK   MTS.

Klamath Falls   GUANO

PLATEAU

CALIFORNIA

CAN
OCEAN